MEDIA COMPOSER® 6:

PART 2—EFFECTS ESSENTIALS

Greg Staten

Course Technology PTR

A part of Cengage Learning

Australia, Brazil, Japan, Korea, Mexico, Singapore, Spain, United Kingdom, United States

COURSE TECHNOLOGY
CENGAGE Learning®

Media Composer® 6:
Part 2—Effects Essentials
Greg Staten

Publisher and General Manager,
Course Technology PTR:
Stacy L. Hiquet

Associate Director of Marketing:
Sarah Panella

Manager of Editorial Services:
Heather Talbot

Senior Marketing Manager:
Mark Hughes

Acquisitions Editor:
Dan Gasparino

Development Editor:
Bryan Castle Jr.

Project Editor:
Kate Shoup

Technical Reviewer:
Phill Naylor

Copy Editor:
Gene Redding

Interior Layout:
Shawn Morningstar

Cover Designer:
Avid Technology, Mike Tanamachi

DVD-ROM Producer:
Avid Technology, Brandon Penticuff

Indexer:
Valerie Haynes Perry

Proofreader:
Kate Shoup

Printed in China
2 3 4 5 6 7 14 13 12

For product information and technology assistance, contact us at
Cengage Learning Customer & Sales Support, 1-800-354-9706

For permission to use material from this text or product,
submit all requests online at **cengage.com/permissions**
Further permissions questions can be emailed to
permissionrequest@cengage.com

Media Composer is a registered trademark of Avid Technology Inc. All other trademarks are the property of their respective owners.

All images © Cengage Learning unless otherwise noted.

Library of Congress Control Number: 2011942187
ISBN-13: 978-1-133-78888-1
ISBN-10: 1-133-78888-2

Course Technology, a part of Cengage Learning
20 Channel Center Street
Boston, MA 02210
USA

Cengage Learning is a leading provider of customized learning solutions with office locations around the globe, including Singapore, the United Kingdom, Australia, Mexico, Brazil, and Japan. Locate your local office at: **international.cengage.com/region**

Cengage Learning products are represented in Canada by Nelson Education, Ltd.

For your lifelong learning solutions, visit **courseptr.com**.

Visit our corporate Web site at **cengage.com**.

This book includes material that was developed in part by the Avid Technical Publications department and the Avid Training department.

For William and Caroline

Acknowledgments

Many thanks to the companies and individuals who provided us with the footage used in this book: NEHST and Allentown Productions for the *Running the Sahara* footage, the Upper Ground Enterprises/Hell's Kitchen post team for the *Hell's Kitchen* footage, and the *Agent Zero* footage (© Brian Barnhart and Thomas Graham 2010).

About the Author

Greg Staten has been editing, consulting, and teaching with Media Composer for nearly 20 years. Previously at Avid, he was the principal instructor within the training group, writing Avid's effects and finishing course books, and speaking and consulting on editing around the world. Later he became the senior product designer for Avid Media Composer and Avid Symphony. Currently at HP, he oversees HP's color critical displays and consults with feature animation and visual effects companies worldwide. He is co-author of *The Avid Handbook, Fifth Edition.*

Contents

Lesson 5
Color Treating and Correcting   99

Exercise 5
Color Treatments and Corrections   119

Lesson 6
Nesting Multiple Effects   121

Exercise 6
Nesting and Order of Processing   135

Lesson 7
Multilayer Effects   137

Exercise 7
Creating Banners and Split Screens   165

Lesson 8
Keying and Mattes   167

Exercise 8
Keying on Different Backgrounds   179

Lesson 9
3D Title Animation with Marquee   181

Exercise 9
Sliding Animation   207

Appendix A
Using AVX Third-Party Plug-ins   209

Appendix B
Performance and Rendering   227

Appendix C
Glossary   245

Appendix D
Answers to Review/Discussion Questions   265

Index   271

Introduction

Welcome to *Media Composer 6: Part 2–Effects Essentials* and the Avid Learning Series. Whether you are interested in self-study or would like to pursue formal certification through an Avid Learning Partner, this book is a key step toward developing your core skills and introduces you to the power of Media Composer 6 effects. In addition, *Media Composer 6: Part 2–Effects Essentials* is the second course of study for those pursuing Media Composer User certification.

The material in this book covers the basic principles and techniques you need to create effects in a Media Composer project. Whether your work involves editing corporate industrials, television programming, Web programming, or independent films, *Media Composer 6: Part 2–Effects Essentials* will teach you what you need to know to be successful with Media Composer.

Using This Book

This book has been designed to familiarize you with the practices and processes you will use to complete a Media Composer project. Each lesson focuses on a different type of effect used in Media Composer, starting with basic transition effects and moving through more advanced effects including Motion effects and keying. Using real-world projects from Media Composer editors, the lessons provide information not only on how the features operate but also the concepts behind them. Media Composer projects and media are provided on the DVD, allowing you to follow step-by-step to perform each task. At the end of each lesson, review questions can help you retain the knowledge you've learned along the way. Additional exercises are also provided, giving you an extra opportunity to explore each feature and technique.

Using the DVD

The DVD-ROM included with this book contains projects and media files for the exercises in the book. These must be installed before you can use them.

If you purchased an ebook version of this book, you may download the contents from www.courseptr.com/downloads. Please note that you will be redirected to the Cengage Learning site.

Installation Instructions

Please follow these installation instructions exactly or you may not have access to all the project files and media associated with this course.

1. Make sure Media Composer 6 is installed and that you have opened the application at least once. Opening the application creates important folders that you will use during this installation.

2. Insert the accompanying DVD into your Windows or Macintosh computer's disc drive.

3. View the contents of the DVD. There are three folders on the DVD, and each folder must be copied to specific locations.

4. Drag the MC6 Effects Book Files folder to your desktop.

5. The Avid MediaFiles and OMFI MediaFiles folders on the DVD contain the individual media files you'll use for this book. These folders should be copied to the top level of your hard drive. If you've already used Media Composer on this system, it is possible that you have existing media folders, which you should not delete.

6. Navigate to the root level of the hard drive where you want to store the media files. This may be your internal drive, in which case navigate to C DRIVE:\ (Windows) or Macintosh HD (Mac). If you have a locally attached external hard drive you want to use, navigate to the root level of the external hard drive.

Note: The root level of a hard drive is also called the top level. It is the highest level in the hierarchy of folders on your computer.

7. Make sure at the top level of your hard drive that there is no existing Avid MediaFiles folder. If there is no existing Avid MediaFiles folder, drag the entire Avid MediaFiles folder from the DVD onto the top level of your hard drive. If an Avid MediaFiles folder does exist on the top level of your hard drive, double-click it to reveal the MXF folder.

8. On the DVD, double-click the Avid MediaFiles folder and then double-click the MXF folder.

9. Inside the DVD's MXF folder are four numbered folders: 110, 111, 112, and 113. Drag all four numbered folders from the DVD into the MXF folder on your hard drive.

10. Make sure at the top level of your hard drive that there is no existing OMFI MediaFiles folder. If there is no existing OMFI MediaFiles folder, drag the entire OMFI MediaFiles folder from the DVD onto the top level of your hard drive. If an OMFI MediaFiles folder does exist on the top level of your hard drive, double-click it to reveal the media files inside.

11. On the DVD, double-click the OMFI MediaFiles folder. Copy media files to the OMFI MediaFiles folder on your hard drive.

Caution: Do not rename the folders named OMFI MediaFiles or Avid MediaFiles located on the media drive. Media Composer uses the folder names to locate the media files.

Prerequisites

This course is designed for those who are new to professional video editing as well as experienced professional editors who are unfamiliar with Media Composer software. Although this book is not aimed at teaching the theory behind film and television editing, the content of this course does provide some background on the craft of editing, making it appropriate for students or people new to the art. At the same time, its primary focus is on how Media Composer works, making it a perfect introduction to the software for skilled professionals.

System Requirements

This book assumes that you have a system configuration suitable to run Media Composer 6. To verify the most recent system requirements, visit www.avid.com/US/products/media-composer and click the System Requirements tab.

Becoming Avid Certified

Avid certification is a tangible, industry-recognized credential that can help you advance your career and provide measurable benefits to your employer. When you're Avid certified, you not only help to accelerate and validate your professional development, but you can also improve your productivity and project success. Avid offers programs supporting certification in dedicated focus areas including Media Composer, Sibelius, Pro Tools, Worksurface Operation, and Live Sound. To become certified in Media Composer, you must enroll in a program at an Avid Learning Partner, where you can complete additional Media Composer coursework if needed and take your certification exam. To locate an Avid Learning Partner, visit www.avid.com/training.

Media Composer Certification

Avid offers two levels of Media Composer certification:

- Avid Media Composer User Certification
- Avid Media Composer Professional Certification

User Certification

The Avid Media Composer Certified User Exam is the first of two certification exams that allow you to become Avid certified. The two combined certifications offer an established and recognized goal for both academic users and industry professionals. The Avid Media Composer User Certification requires that you display a firm grasp of the core skills, workflows, and concepts of non-linear editing on the Media Composer system.

Courses/books associated with User certification include the following:

- *Media Composer 6: Part 1–Editing Essentials* (MC101)
- *Media Composer 6: Part 2–Effects Essentials* (MC110)

These User courses can be complemented with *Color Grading with Media Composer 6 and Symphony 6.*

Professional Certification

The Avid Media Composer Professional Certification prepares editors to competently operate a Media Composer system in a professional production environment. Professional certification requires a more advanced understanding of Media Composer, including advanced tools and workflows involved in creating professional programs.

Courses/books associated with Professional certification include the following:

- *Media Composer 6: Professional Picture and Sound Editing* (MC201)
- *Media Composer 6: Professional Effects and Compositing* (MC205)

These Professional courses can be complemented with *Color Grading with Media Composer 6 and Symphony 6.*

For more information about Avid's certification program, please visit www.avid.com/US/support/training/certification.

Introduction to Audio Effects

This lesson covers some of the core AudioSuite plug-ins included with Media Composer that perform a wide range of signal-processing to improve your sound design. In fact, it's often said that 50 percent of your audience's experience will come from audio, so understanding when, how, and why you use audio signal processing plug-ins can make or break your piece.

Media Used: Hell's Kitchen

Duration: 60 minutes

GOALS

- Use the Audio EQ tool
- Explore AudioSuite plug-ins
- Apply AudioSuite to a master clip

Audio EQ Tool

You've probably used an equalizer before if you've ever adjusted the bass or treble frequency on your stereo or car radio. Although a bit more advanced, the Audio EQ (equalization) tool in Media Composer lets you boost or cut the bass, midrange, and treble frequencies of an audio clip. It also includes a number of EQ presets that make it easy to get commonly used EQ settings without a lot of fiddling.

In this lesson, you'll use a scene from the reality cooking competition television series *Hell's Kitchen*. First, you'll EQ some dialogue and then learn about AudioSuite plug-ins and all the sound design tools built into Media Composer.

To prepare to use the Audio EQ tool:

1. Open Media Composer. The Avid Projects folder should be located on your desktop if you followed the installation instructions, so they won't show in the Select a Project list by default.

2. Click the **BROWSE** button. (See Figure 1.1.) The Browse for Folder (Windows) or Project Directory (Mac) dialog box opens.

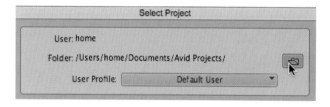

Figure 1.1

Click the Browse button and navigate to the Avid Projects folder on your desktop.

3. Navigate to and select the **AVID PROJECTS** folder located on your desktop, then click **OK** (Windows) or **OPEN** (Mac).

4. Select **HELL'S KITCHEN PT2** in the Projects list and click **OK**. The Project window opens and lists all the bins associated with this project. The bin you'll use in this lesson is HK Audio FX, which contains sequences you'll use throughout this lesson.

5. Double-click the **HK AUDIO FX** bin in the Project window.

6. In the bin that opens, double-click **HK AUDIOFX START**. The sequence appears in the Record monitor (see Figure 1.2). This is a scene from the *Hell's Kitchen* television show.

7. Whenever you begin working on a sequence, you should always watch it to get an understanding of the content. Place the position indicator at the start of the sequence by pressing the **HOME** key on the keyboard. (If you are on a Mac without a Home key, press the **FUNCTION+LEFT ARROW** keyboard shortcut.)

Figure 1.2
Viewing the HK AudioFX-START sequence in the Record monitor.

8. Press the **SPACE BAR** to play the sequence until the end. As you view the sequence, take particular notice of the dialogue and voiceover narration.

9. When done listening to the sequence, place the position indicator over the first segment on tracks A1 and A2, as shown in Figure 1.3. This is the first dialogue with Chef Ramsay.

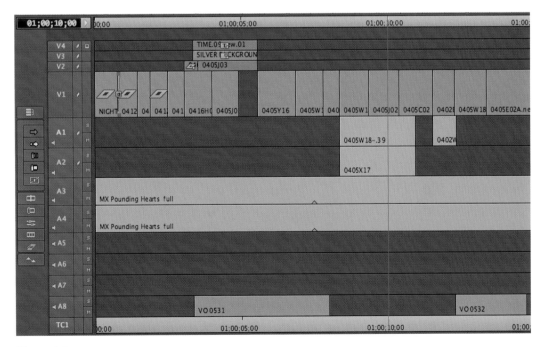

Figure 1.3
Place the position indicator over the first segment on tracks A1 and A2.

10. Select tracks **A1** and **A2** and make sure all other tracks are deselected, and then click the **MARK CLIP** button or press **T** to set IN and OUT points around the clips.

11. To clearly hear your EQ, it's best to solo the tracks. Click the **SOLO** buttons for tracks A1 and A2 (see Figure 1.4).

Figure 1.4
Solo tracks A1 and A2.

To use the Audio EQ tool:

1. With A1 and A2 selected and marked, select **TOOLS > AUDIO EQ**. The Audio EQ tool opens. (See Figure 1.5.) The Audio EQ tool provides three "bands" of EQ: The left slider is the bass or low shelf, which affects all low frequencies from 240 Hz to 50 Hz and below. The far right slider is the treble or high shelf, which affects all high frequencies from 6 kHz to 20 kHz and higher. The middle slider is the midrange, which affects frequencies between the low shelf and the high shelf as narrow as ¼ octave or as wide as two octaves.

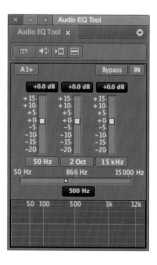

Figure 1.5
The Audio EQ tool provides three bands of EQ: low shelf, midrange and high shelf.

Note: Audio EQ is applied only to an entire segment or to multiple segments between IN and OUT points. To affect portions of a segment, you can use the Add Edit button to create smaller segments.

What Is an Octave?

Vibrations in the air, called *frequencies*, cause sound. If there are 240 vibrations, the sound is described as being at 240 *hertz* (Hz). The lower the Hz, the lower the pitch. The higher Hz, the higher the pitch. When adjusting EQ, the low, mid, and high bands are determined by the range of frequencies that they adjust. The midrange EQ can be as wide as two octaves. An *octave* is the range between two pitches, one of which is twice the frequency of the other. A sound at the frequency of 240 Hz is an octave lower than a sound at the frequency of 480 Hz.

2. Click the Audio EQ tool **FAST MENU** button and select **SET EQ IN/OUT** (see Figure 1.6) to apply any adjustments to the marked segments.

Figure 1.6

From the Fast menu, select Set EQ IN/OUT.

3. To play the currently selected audio clip, click the **AUDIO LOOP PLAY** button from the basic tools in the upper part of the EQ window. Click it again after you have heard the entire clip.

Tip: If no IN and OUT points are set, the Fast menu option applies the EQ effect to the entire tracks that are selected.

4. The Audio EQ tool Fast menu provides access to a number of predefined EQ templates. Click the Audio EQ tool **FAST MENU** button and choose **MALE VOICE WITH PRESENCE**, as shown in Figure 1.7. An EQ icon appears on the Timeline segment that was selected, indicating that an EQ effect is applied.

5. Click the **AUDIO LOOP PLAY** button to hear the applied template.

6. While the audio plays, click the **BYPASS** button to listen to the original audio and then click **BYPASS** again to hear the change.

Tip: Depending on your system performance, it may take a few seconds for the changes to be heard as you adjust the EQ. You can improve the response time by not monitoring the video track.

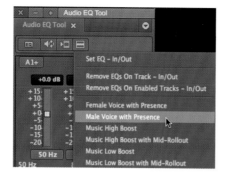

Figure 1.7
Choose Male Voice with
Presence from the Fast menu.

7. If you aren't happy with the templates, you can return to the EQ adjustments and set the EQ yourself. Click the **OVERRIDE WITH DEFAULT EQ** button. The EQ tool returns to display the EQ parameter adjustments.

8. As a general rule, when dialogue or narration will be over a soundtrack, it's best to aim for a thinner-sounding EQ (less bass, more treble and midrange). Click the **MIDRANGE** slider and drag it up, boosting it by 10 or 15 dB. (See Figure 1.8.) It's helpful to boost a slider significantly at first, to hear the change more noticeably. The bottom half of the Audio EQ tool shows a frequency response curve. As you make adjustments, the horizontal center line of the frequency response curve moves above the zero line (or below if you drag the slider down), indicating that the corresponding frequencies are emphasized.

Figure 1.8
Drag the Midrange slider up by 10 or 15 dB.

Tip: The human voice has a frequency range of approximately 100–5,000 Hz. As a general guideline, if you have a person with a nasal voice on camera, try to deemphasize the 1 KHz range; for bothersome plosives and rumblings, deemphasize below 100 Hz; and to add clarity, boost the range above 2 KHz. Above all, don't use EQ just because you can; use it with a goal in mind.

9. The center slider you adjusted is a sweepable midrange slider. The horizontal slider under the three EQ sliders (see Figure 1.9) is called the Frequency Range slider, and it is used to set the midrange anywhere within a wide frequency range. To add more clarity or presence, place the FREQUENCY RANGE slider around **2,500 Hz**.

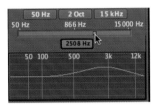

Figure 1.9
Drag the Frequency Range slider to around 2,500 Hz.

10. After adjusting different areas of the midrange, return the slider to the zero setting. Then start boosting the slider in small steps until you reach what you consider to be the best sound, somewhere around 5 dB.

11. The EQ you have created can probably be used for other dialogue in this program. To reuse this EQ on other segments, you can save it as an EQ effect setting. To save EQ settings, drag the effect icon in the upper left of the Audio EQ tool (see Figure 1.10) to the **HK AUDIO SOURCE CLIPS** bin. Once you have saved an EQ effect to a bin, you can drag the effect icon from the bin to any audio segments in the Timeline.

Figure 1.10
Drag the effect icon in the Audio EQ tool to a bin to save it as an effect.

Tip: You can remove audio EQ effects with the Audio EQ tool Fast menu, with the Remove Effect button, or by selecting the segment with the Segment Smart tool and pressing the Delete key. You will learn more about removing effects in Lesson 2, "Introduction to Visual Effects."

12. Close the Audio EQ tool and disable the **SOLO** button on both the A1 and A2 tracks.

13. Place the position indicator at the start of the sequence by pressing the **HOME** key on the keyboard. (If you are on a Mac without a Home key, press the **FUNCTION+LEFT ARROW** keyboard shortcut.)

14. Press the **SPACE BAR** to play the sequence through your EQ-affected segments.

You now have clear-sounding dialogue that cuts through the music. Although EQ might be the most common audio processing used in post-production, Media Composer includes a number of other options that can improve your sound design as well. Those other options are included as audio plug-ins called AudioSuite.

Understanding AudioSuite Plug-ins

Once you get beyond level, pan, and the basic three-band EQ controls, all of Media Composer's audio processing is handled by AudioSuite plug-ins. AudioSuite, Avid's audio plug-in standard, opens up your audio processing to plug-ins developed by Avid and by third-party developers. From fix-it style plug-ins like noise removal and time compression/expansion to creative delays and lo-fi sound simulators, plug-ins perform a wide range of audio processes for post-production. Media Composer includes over three dozen audio-processing effects, and there are many more to choose from if you want to expand your options. To start, let's highlight a few AudioSuite plug-ins and their uses; then we'll work with some of the most popular ones.

■ **BF Essential Clip Remover.** If audio isn't monitored constantly during production, it can exceed the maximum level of your recording device. This can cause *clipping*, which is when the loudest peaks of audio are not even recorded, they are just "clipped" off. The BF Essential Clip Remover, shown in Figure 1.11, repairs clipped audio recordings, potentially saving you from having to re-record.

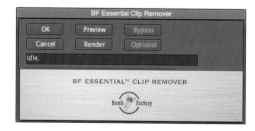

Figure 1.11
BF Essential Clip Remover repairs clipped audio recordings.

■ **De-Esser Dyn 3.** High-frequency noises that can occur from "ess" and "shh" sounds in narration can cause peaks in an audio signal and lead to distortion. The De-Esser Dyn 3 plug-in, shown in Figure 1.12, reduces these unwanted sounds to produce a smoother voiceover.

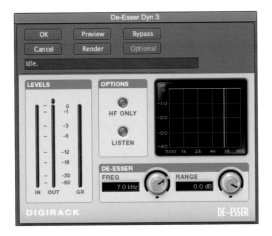

Figure 1.12

The De-Esser Dyn 3 plug-in reduces high-frequency noises like "ess" and "shh" sounds in narration.

■ **D-Verb.** Digital reverberation processing can simulate natural reflections and echoes of sound that occur in different-sized rooms. Reverberation can take relatively dull source material and create an environment that gives audio a perceived weight and depth in a mix. D-Verb, shown in Figure 1.13, provides control over these reverberation parameters so that extremely natural-sounding reverb effects can be produced.

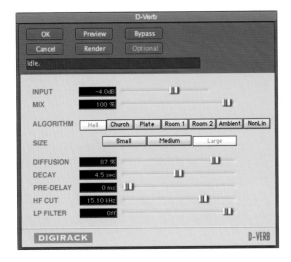

Figure 1.13

D-Verb can simulate natural reflections of sound that occur in different-sized rooms.

■ **Expander/Gate Dyn 3.** Expanders operate on low-level audio to make quiet sounds quieter. A threshold is set, and any noise below that threshold is decreased. It is most often used as a form of noise reduction, and that is why it is combined with the Gate function, which is a more heavy-handed noise-reduction tool. (See Figure 1.14.)

Figure 1.14
Expanders operate as a form of noise reduction on low-level audio.

■ **Normalize.** Normalize raises the peak of the audio signal as high as it can be without distortion; the remaining audio signal is adjusted by the same amount. Normalize is used when volume faders can't make a quiet segment loud enough and re-recording is not an option. (See Figure 1.15.) But be warned, Normalize increases the signal and therefore increases the noise.

Figure 1.15
Normalize raises the peak of the audio signal as high as it can be without distortion.

RTAS

Media Composer supports a second type of AudioSuite plug-in called Real-Time AudioSuite, or RTAS. RTAS plug-ins are audio effects that you apply to tracks rather than to segments within your sequence. Unlike AudioSuite plug-ins, RTAS plug-ins are processed on tracks in real time, without being rendered first. This lets you add a type of audio track effect that is supported in all versions of Avid Pro Tools.

When you use more than one plug-in on a track, Media Composer processes them in a series. Each effect is added to any previous effect (moving from left to right in the Track Control panel).

Avid qualifies a number of RTAS plug-ins manufactured by Avid for use with the current version of Media Composer. Avid also supports some plug-ins from third-party vendors that you can purchase separately. To explore additional audio plug-ins for purchase, choose Media Composer Marketplace > Audio Plugins.

If you move your sequence from one Avid editing application to another system and the RTAS plug-in is not installed on that system, "Unavailable Effect," the name of the effect, and other information appears in the RTAS tool.

Using AudioSuite Plug-ins

Now that you understand what AudioSuite is and some of the more essential plug-ins, let's put a couple of the most popular ones into action. The Compressor/Limiter Dyn 3 plug-in automatically adjusts the audio signals that exceed a specific threshold in order to smooth out volume changes. A classic example of when to use a compressor/limiter is an interview on camera with the person wearing a lavalier microphone. Every time the interviewee looks down, the volume increases because his mouth moves closer to the microphone. In our sequence, the compressor/limiter can help with the more subtle variations in the narration.

To use the Compressor/Limiter Dyn 3 plug-in:

1. Place the position indicator at the start of the sequence then press the SPACE BAR to play the sequence until you reach the end of the second narration sentence, "But Chef Ramsay is a little suspicious." (See Figure 1.16.)

Figure 1.16
Play through the second narration line "But Chef Ramsay is a little suspicious."

2. After listening to the sequence, place the position indicator over the second narration segment on track A8.

3. Select track **A8** and make sure all other tracks are deselected, and then click the **MARK CLIP** button or press **T** to set IN and OUT points around the segment.

4. Solo track A8 so you are not distracted by the music tracks.

5. Choose **TOOLS > AUDIOSUITE** to open the AudioSuite window.

6. To apply the Compressor/Limiter Dyn 3 AudioSuite plug-in, choose it from the plug-in selection menu. (See Figure 1.17.)

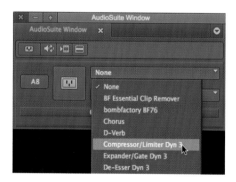

Figure 1.17
Choose Compressor/Limiter Dyn 3 from the plug-in selection menu.

7. To open the dialog box for the plug-in, click the **ACTIVATE CURRENT PLUG-IN** button, shown in Figure 1.18.

Figure 1.18
Click the Activate Current Plug-in
button to open the dialog box.

8. The plug-in dialog box opens, showing the controls for the particular plug-in. (See Figure 1.19.) Although the Compressor/Limiter controls appear intimidating, there are two primary controls: Ratio and Thresh (short for Threshold). The Ratio knob displays ratios—1:1, 2:1, 3:1, etc. The ratio reflects how many input decibels are needed to produce one decibel of change in the output. A very high ratio setting would flatten all of the dynamics. For speech, a ratio from 2:1 to 4:1 will give the right amount of compression while still sounding natural. Drag the **RATIO** knob to about **4.0:1**.

Figure 1.19
Drag the Ratio knob to 4.0:1 to add natural-sounding compression for narration.

9. To hear the change, click the **PREVIEW** button at the top of the Compressor/Limiter dialog box. Once the entire narration is played, click the **BYPASS** button to hear the original audio. Click **BYPASS** again to return to the affected audio.

10. Thresh will set the point at which the compressor will start to kick in. By setting Thresh, you can choose to have the compressor start working on low volumes or work when the volume gets loud. Drag the **THRESH** knob to about **−30 DB** to lower the threshold for compression. (See Figure 1.20.)

Figure 1.20
Drag the Thresh knob to −30 dB to set the trigger point for the compression.

11. To hear the change, click the **PREVIEW** button at the top of the Compressor/Limiter dialog box. Once it has played through the entire narration, click the **BYPASS** button to hear the original audio. Click **BYPASS** again to return to the affected audio.

12. The Compression settings have the side effect of lowering the volume of the audio segment. Increase the **GAIN** knob to between roughly **6.0** and **7.0 DB** to compensate for the compression. As you preview the segment, watch the Output level meters on the left side of the dialog box to ensure the peak signal levels are still well below 0 dB after increasing the gain. (See Figure 1.21.)

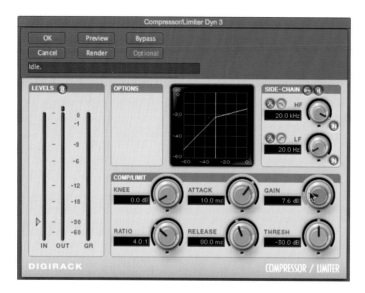

Figure 1.21
Increase the Gain knob to 7.0 dB to compensate for the compression.

13. Unlike RTAS plug-ins, AudioSuite plug-ins need to be rendered to play in the sequence. Rendering creates a file on disk for the affected portion of the clip, which is then used to play in the sequence. Click the **RENDER** button at the top of the Compressor/Limiter Dyn 3 dialog box to render the effect. In the Render Effect dialog box, select the drive where you want to store the file, and then click **OK**.

14. Close the Compressor/Limiter Dyn 3 dialog box and then close the AudioSuite window.

15. Click the **SOLO** button on track A8 and press the **SPACE BAR** to hear the full mix with the newly compressed audio.

When you have the AudioSuite plug-in applied to your sequence, the segment will have an audio plug-in icon. The icon indicates you have a plug-in effect on the segment, making it easy to locate the segments with AudioSuite processing applied.

Applying AudioSuite Plug-ins to Master Clips

You can use AudioSuite plug-ins on master clips as well as on segments in a sequence. Applying an AudioSuite plug-in to a master clip lets you change the length of the media specifically for effects that perform time compression and expansion. For example, you can use a time compression/expansion plug-in to slow down the clip, thereby extending its duration, or you can lengthen the file in order to add a reverb trail. Let's examine the use of the Time Shift plug-in on a master clip. The Time Shift plug-in can be a lifesaver when your voiceover talent is a slow or fast talker or if you want a deeper tone. The high-quality algorithm lets you adjust the duration of selected segments with or without changing pitch. Narration or even music can be adjusted to specific time lengths or timecode durations for synchronization.

To apply AudioSuite plug-ins to master clips:

1. Place the position indicator at the start of the sequence, then press the **SPACE BAR** to play the sequence until you reach the end of the first narration sentence, "It's an hour into dinner service, and the blue team has just delivered their first entrée."

2. This narration sounds a little rushed. Let's check to see if there is room in the sequence for this narration to last longer. Place the position indicator over the first narration segment on track A8. Select track **A8** and make sure all other tracks are deselected, then click the **MARK CLIP** button or press **T** to mark the clip.

3. Drag the position indicator past the end of the narration until Chef Ramsay comes on screen. This is the point where the dialogue on tracks A1 and A2 begins, so we cannot go any further than this point with the narration—roughly 01:29:11:13. (See Figure 1.22.)

4. Mark an OUT point. The center duration display at the top of the Composer window shows it is roughly 5:00 from the IN point to the OUT point. So that is how much we can extend the duration of the clip.

5. In the Hell's Kitchen Project window, double-click the **HK AUDIO SOURCE CLIPS** bin to open it.

Figure 1.22
Drag the position indicator to the point where Chef Ramsay comes on screen.

6. Choose **Tools > AudioSuite** to open the AudioSuite window.

7. From the HK Audio Source Clips bin, drag the **VO 05 32** clip onto the AudioSuite window.

Tip: You can drag more than one clip onto the window and then select the clip you want to work with through the Clip Selection menu.

8. To apply the Time Shift AudioSuite plug-in, choose it from the plug-in selection menu, then open the dialog box for the plug-in by clicking the **Activate Current Plug-in** button, shown in Figure 1.23.

Figure 1.23
Choose the Time Shift plug-in and then click the Activate Current Plug-in button.

9. The Mode menu at the top of the Time Shift dialog box allows you to select the type of material you are working with. In this case it is narration, so choose **MONOPHONIC** from the **MODE** menu, as shown in Figure 1.24.

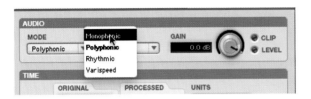

Figure 1.24
Choose Monophonic from the Mode menu when you are operating on dialogue or narration.

10. To change the clip's length, rotate the **SPEED** knob until speed is at around **87%**, as shown in Figure 1.25.

Figure 1.25
Set the Speed knob to around 87%.

11. Click the **PREVIEW** button at the top of the dialog box to preview the effect. After you listen to the preview play once or twice, click the **BYPASS** button to compare the original pace of the narration. Click the **BYPASS** button again to hear the affected narration. The narration is slightly slower, but the pitch of the voice is the same.

12. You can make adjustments while you are previewing the clip. Let's adjust the pitch of the voice independently of the speed using the Pitch knob. We'll give the narrator a slightly deeper voice. Drag the **PITCH** knob until the Shift field displays about **85%**, as shown in Figure 1.26.

Figure 1.26
Set the Pitch knob to around 85% to create a deeper-sounding voice.

13. When Pitch is set, click the **PREVIEW** button to stop listening to the preview.

14. To complete the process, a new clip must be created at the new pitch and speed. Click the **OK** button at the top of the Time Shift dialog box, then in the AudioSuite window choose **HK AUDIO SOURCE CLIPS** as the bin where you want to save the new clip, as shown in Figure 1.27.

Figure 1.27
Choose HK Audio Source Clips as the bin where you want to save the new clip.

15. Click the **RENDER** button at the top of the AudioSuite window to start rendering, as shown in Figure 1.28.

Figure 1.28
Click the Render button to create the new clip.

When you click the Render button, Media Composer creates a new master clip in the target bin. It then names the new master clip by combining the original clip name with the effect name. The new master clip is ready to be edited into your sequence at any time.

Review/Discussion Questions

1. Where do you find the Audio EQ window?

2. The Audio EQ tool is which of the following?

   a. A midrange band EQ

   b. A four-band EQ

   c. A three-band EQ

3. True or false: AudioSuite plug-ins are real-time plug-ins that do not require rendering.

4. Why would you use a compressor/limiter?

5. True or false: AudioSuite plug-ins can be applied only to segments in a sequence.

6. While listening to the affected clip in an AudioSuite plug-in, which button do you click to listen to the original audio?

   a. Activate Current Plug-in

   b. Bypass

   c. Threshold

Lesson 1 Keyboard Shortcut

Key	Shortcut
Home (Windows)/Function+Left Arrow (Mac)	**Move to start of Timeline**

Using EQ and a Compressor/Limiter

On the same sequence you have been using, add EQ to the remaining dialogue on tracks A1 and A2. Then edit the new time-shifted segment into the sequence and add a compressor to it.

Media Used:

Hell's Kitchen

Duration:

15 minutes

GOAL

■ Apply EQ and compressor/limiter plug-ins

Adding EQ

1. Return to the **HK Audio-START** sequence that you were working on earlier.

2. On the remaining A1 dialogue segments, add EQ to multiple clips by marking IN and OUT points around the clips you want to affect.

3. Use the **Fast** menu in the Audio EQ tool to add a preset to the segments.

4. Render it and listen to your results.

Applying a Compressor

1. Replace the first narration segment on track A8 with the newly created time-shifted clip in the Audio Source Clips bin.

2. Once the segment is in the sequence, add a compressor to it to smooth out the variations of the audio level.

3. Render it and listen to your results.

Introduction to Visual Effects

After you've assembled and refined a sequence, the next phase in a workflow often involves adding effects to the picture. Even in the most straightforward of projects, visual effects can play an important role in the timing and dramatic feel of a sequence. As an editor, it's just as important for you to learn why you add effects as it is to learn the steps to apply them. In this project, you'll start with the fundamental steps, and cover a few "whys" along the way.

Media Used: Running the Sahara

Duration: 30 minutes

GOALS

- Apply Quick Transitions
- Modify transitions in the Timeline
- Remove effects
- Create and apply effect templates
- Understand the different effect types
- Add and remove segment effects

Adding Quick Transitions

Media Composer uses the same basic method to create crossfades for audio and dissolves for pictures. Because these are the most commonly used effects, they get special privileges, like a super-quick way to be added to a sequence. Let's look at a simple cuts-only sequence and enhance it by quickly adding a few visual transition effects.

To add visual transition effects:

1. If the Running the Sahara project is not open from the last lesson, launch Media Composer, select the **RUNNING THE SAHARA** project on the left side of the Open Project dialog box, and click the **OPEN** button. The Project window opens and lists all the bins associated with this project.

2. The bin you'll use in this lesson is the RTS PT2 FX Sequences bin, which contains a number of sequences you'll use throughout this book. Double-click the **RTS PT2 FX SEQUENCES** bin in the Project window to open it, as shown in Figure 2.1.

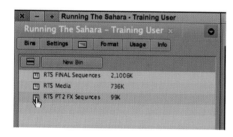

Figure 2.1
Opening the RTS PT2 FX Sequences bin in the Project window.

3. In the RTS PT2 FX Sequences bin window, double-click the **RTS FX PT2 LESSON 02** sequence. The sequence appears in the Record monitor, as shown in Figure 2.2.

4. Before you add transitions, watch a few seconds of the trailer to get a feel for the project. To place the position indicator at the start of the project, press the **HOME** key on your keyboard. (If you use a Mac with no Home key, press the **FUNCTION+LEFT ARROW** keyboard shortcut.)

5. Press the **SPACE BAR** to play back the project, and watch it all the way through. If you read *Media Composer 6: Part I–Editing Essentials*, then this trailer is familiar to you. (If you jumped directly to this book, slap your hand and glare at yourself with disappointment because there are fundamentals taught in that book that we will refer to here.) This portion of the trailer is the opening montage, which introduces the setting: the Sahara. For such a mysterious opening, it lacks a bit of drama. Not only can transitions add drama, they can also improve flow by smoothing abrupt cuts. You'll start by adding a transition to the first cut in the project.

Figure 2.2
The sequence opens in the Record monitor.

6. Because you want to apply the transition to the video track, make sure **V1** is selected in the Track Selector panel. If necessary, deselect the A1, A2, A3, and A4 audio tracks, as shown in Figure 2.3.

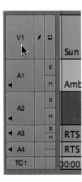

Figure 2.3
Selecting the V1 track.

7. Place the position indicator at the start of the project by pressing the **HOME** key on the keyboard. (If you use a Mac with no Home key, press the **FUNCTION+LEFT ARROW** keyboard shortcut.)

8. Press the **S** key. This moves the position indicator to the first transition, placing you in Trim mode on the cut point where you will add the transition effect.

9. Click the **Quick Transition** button in the Timeline toolbar, as shown in Figure 2.4, or press the **\ (backslash)** key on the keyboard. The Quick Transition dialog box opens. You'll use this dialog box to add a dissolve transition to this first cut.

Figure 2.4
The Quick Transition button.

10. In the Quick Transition dialog box, shown in Figure 2.5, make sure the **Position** drop-down menu is set to the default, **Starting at Cut**. (You'll understand why in a moment.)

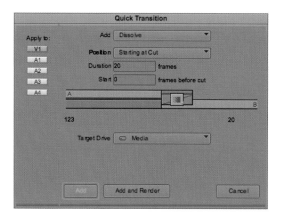

Figure 2.5
Entering transition settings.

11. Type **36** in the **Duration** field. Because this is a 24 fps project, typing 36 in the Duration field creates a 1.5-second transition. Note, however, that when you type 36, Media Composer changes it to 20. No, it's not due to the lack of math and science taught in schools these days. To create a transition, adequate source media must exist beyond what is edited into the sequence. This extra media is referred to as *handle*. If you attempt to add a transition where there is not enough handle, Media Composer automatically adjusts to give you the longest possible transition. You can accept the new duration or change the alignment of the transition to allow for the longer duration.

Note: As shown in Figure 2.5, the Quick Transition dialog box includes a scaled
graphical display of the transition that shows the alignment and handles.
This can help you to understand the duration and handle problem. Since the
transition starts at the cut point, there must be 36 additional frames for the
outgoing (A side) shot. But Media Composer changed the duration to 20, so
you now know there are only 20 frames of handle on the A side. Changing
the alignment so the transition is centered on the cut instead of starting
at the cut means there only need to be 18 frames of handle on the A side
and B side.

12. In the Quick Transition dialog box, click the **Position** drop-down menu
and choose **Centered on Cut**. Then type **36** in the **Duration** field, as
shown in Figure 2.6. The transition now fits with the desired duration.

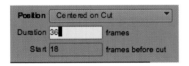

Figure 2.6
Reconfiguring the transition settings.

Tip: Another way to adjust a transition is to drag the left or right edge of the purple
box in the Quick Transition dialog box to change its duration or drag within
the purple box to change its position.

13. Click the **Add** button or press **Return** (Mac) or **Enter** (Windows) to add
the default dissolve transition and close the Quick Transition dialog box. The
transition is indicated in the sequence by a Dissolve icon in the Timeline.

Note: Because Quick Transitions are real-time effects, you only need to click the
Add button. If you were to click the Add and Render button, Media Composer
would render the transition, creating a new media file on your hard drive. If
you want to guarantee real-time playback on older systems, you can choose
to render Quick Transitions, but you must also choose a storage location for
the rendered media file. The Quick Transition dialog box allows you to choose
where to store the media for rendered transitions. The default is the Effect
Source drive, which is specified in the Render tab of the Media Creation
settings.

14. Watch the transition to see if it improved the cut. Click the **Play Loop**
button under the Record monitor (see Figure 2.7) to loop the playback of
the transition. Click it again to stop playback after you have reviewed the
transition a few times.

Figure 2.7
Play back the transition.

15. The transition smoothes out the cut, but because this is a major introduction point where the narration starts, it might be better with a dramatic pause. To modify the existing transition to improve the feel of the opening, click the **QUICK TRANSITION** button or press the \ (**BACKSLASH**) key on the keyboard while in Trim mode to reopen the Quick Transition dialog box.

16. Although dissolves are the most commonly used type of transition, there are other options in the Quick Transition dialog box that might work better. In the dialog box, click the **ADD** drop-down menu and choose **DIP TO COLOR**, as shown in Figure 2.8. Then click the **ADD** button. This replaces the dissolve with a dip-to-color transition, as indicated by the change of icons in the Timeline. With the dip-to-color transition, the screen fades from the outgoing clip to a color (black by default), and then fades in from the color to the incoming clip. This fade will give the narration more emphasis as it comes in.

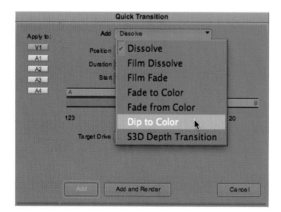

Figure 2.8
Choosing the Dip to Color transition.

17. To review the dip-to-color transition, click the **PLAY LOOP** button under the Record monitor. Click it again to stop playback after you have reviewed the transition. Finally, press the **ESC** key to leave Trim mode.

The first cut is much better with the dip-to-color transition. It sets the right tone for the trailer. Maintaining the right tone or feeling in a project is certainly a major factor to keep in mind when you are deciding to add any effect!

Adding a Transition to Multiple Cuts

The next few cuts after the first transition make up the opening scenic montage. To make this series of cuts feel more unified with the first transition, add transitions to the next four cut points. Instead of adding transitions one by one, you can quickly add transitions to multiple cut points at once using the Quick Transition dialog box.

To add a transition to multiple cuts:

1. In the Timeline, place the position indicator just after the dip-to-color transition.

2. To add multiple Quick Transitions to a group of cut points, the first step is to place them between a mark IN point and a mark OUT point. To begin, click the **MARK IN** button, shown in Figure 2.9, or press the **I** key on the keyboard.

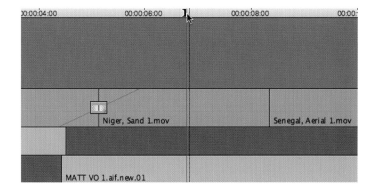

Figure 2.9
The Mark IN button.

3. Drag the position indicator to the sixth segment in the project, **WOMAN WITH BAG ON HEAD** (see Figure 2.10). Then click the **MARK OUT** button or press **O** on the keyboard.

Figure 2.10
The Woman with Bag on Head segment.

4. Now you can use the Quick Transition dialog box to add the effect. Instead of going to Trim mode, however, you need only place the position indicator near one of the transitions within the mark IN and mark OUT range. Drag the position indicator back to the segment before Woman with Bag on Head (**SAND 3**). Then click the **QUICK TRANSITION** button or press the \ (**BACKSLASH**) key to open the Quick Transition dialog box.

5. In the **DURATION** field, type **24** to create a one-second transition. Then click the **POSITION** drop-down menu and choose **CENTERED ON CUT**.

6. Enable the **APPLY TO ALL TRANSITIONS (IN->OUT)** check box, as shown in Figure 2.11.

Figure 2.11
Enabling the Apply to All Transitions (IN->OUT) check box.

7. Click the **ADD** button. All the cuts within the mark IN and mark OUT range now have a one-second dissolve transition applied. Watch the sequence to review the effects.

8. Press the **G** key to clear the mark IN and mark OUT points from the Timeline.

9. Press the **HOME** key to place the position indicator at the start of the project. (If you use a Mac with no Home key, press the **FUNCTION+LEFT ARROW** keyboard shortcut.)

10. Press the **SPACE BAR** to play the sequence. Press it again to stop playback after you view the last transition added.

Most of these transitions look good. They create a smooth, dramatic introduction to the trailer. Still, there are always improvements to be made, as you'll see in the next section.

Removing Transitions

Experience from viewing your uncle's home movies tells you that not every transition you add will improve your sequence. Remember what I said about setting a tone? Often, a straight cut can set the tone and pacing better than a transition effect. That's the case with the last transition.

To remove transitions:

1. Press the **HOME** key to place the position indicator at the start of the project. (If you use a Mac with no Home key, press the **FUNCTION+LEFT ARROW** keyboard shortcut.)

2. Press the **SPACE BAR** to play the sequence. Press it again to stop playback after you view the last transition. As you probably noticed, the sequence suddenly changes from a montage of scenic shots to a very arresting shot of an exotic women (well, exotic assuming you are not from Saharan Africa). This is shown in Figure 2.12. The trailer changes tone, almost as if one paragraph were ending and another beginning. The smooth transition de-emphasizes this dramatic change, so let's try removing it.

Figure 2.12
The sequence changes from a montage of scenic shots to a shot of a woman.

3. Place the position indicator directly over the last transition in the Timeline.

4. Click the **REMOVE EFFECT** button (see Figure 2.13) or press **SHIFT+** (**BACKSLASH**). The dissolve is removed from the Timeline.

Figure 2.13
The Remove Effect button.

5. Press the **HOME** key to place the position indicator at the start of the project. (If you use a Mac with no Home key, press the **FUNCTION+LEFT ARROW** keyboard shortcut.)

6. Press the **SPACE BAR** to play the sequence. Press it again to stop playback after Matt Damon says, "With people and cultures as unpredictable as the landscape." Notice that the change is much better. You can feel the pace quicken and how the introduction of people is more dramatic.

Modifying Transitions in the Timeline

Once you have transitions in the Timeline, you don't have to open the Quick Transition dialog box to make modifications. Some changes, like duration and alignment, can be done directly in the Timeline.

The dissolve from the Senegal Aerial shot to the Sand 3 shot is too long. It takes away from the already short Senegal Aerial shot. To correct this, shorten the transition's length and change its alignment to see more of the Senegal Aerial shot. You'll make those changes directly in the Timeline.

To modify transitions:

1. In the Smart Tool palette, click the **TRANSITION MANIPULATION** button, as shown in Figure 2.14. The Transition Manipulation tool enables you to lengthen, shorten, or move a transition by dragging the effect icon in the Timeline.

Figure 2.14
The Transition Manipulation button.

2. In the Timeline, position the mouse pointer over the transition between the **SENEGAL AERIAL 3** shot and the **SAND 3** shot until a hand icon appears, as shown in Figure 2.15. The hand icon indicates that you can change the alignment of the transition by dragging it. In this case, you want to drag it further to the right, adding more duration to the Senegal Aerial shot.

Figure 2.15
The hand icon.

3. In the Timeline, drag the **DISSOLVE** icon to the right, as shown in Figure 2.16. As you drag, the Record monitor changes to the Transition Corner display, which shows the first, middle, and last frames of the A and B sides of the transition (see Figure 2.17). You can use these frames to guide you as you modify the effect. The six frames shown make it easy to remove an unintended cut or flash frame in the handle of an effect. This is especially common on programs where an edit master is used as one of the source tapes.

Figure 2.16
Dragging the Dissolve icon.

First frame of transition   Center frame of transition   Last frame of transition

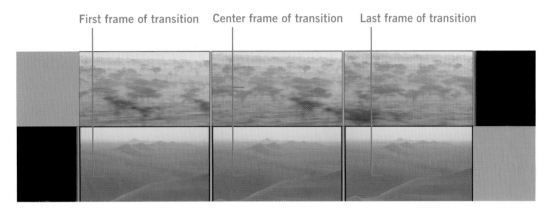

Figure 2.17
The Transition Corner display.

4. Release the mouse button when the transition is all the way to the right of the cut point. The dissolve is repositioned to start at the cut.

Note: You cannot drag an effect beyond the cut point, nor can you drag an effect beyond the ends of the handles.

5. You can also use the Transition Manipulation tool to change the duration of a transition. In the Timeline, position the mouse pointer over the top-right corner of the transition until the mouse pointer changes to a resizing arrow.

6. Drag the transition handle to the left to shorten the duration to about 15 frames, as shown in Figure 2.18. The duration of the transition is displayed under the left side of the Transition Corner display. Note that because you are dragging from the right side of the transition, you are changing where the transition ends. If you were to drag from the lower-left corner of the transition, you would change where the transition starts. In either case, the Transition Corner display appears to assist you in selecting the frames to include in the dissolve.

Figure 2.18
Shortening the duration of the clip.

Tip: You can press the Alt key (Windows) or the Option key (Mac) before you drag a transition handle to lengthen or shorten the transition equally in both directions.

7. Play the sequence to review the changes made to this transition. Click the **PLAY LOOP** button under the Record monitor to loop the playback of the transition. Click it again to stop playback after you have reviewed the transition a few times.

8. Click the **TRANSITION MANIPULATION** tool to disable it.

These changes work well. You now see more of the Senegal Aerial shot before the transition occurs. But because this is the end of the scenic montage, it might be better to end it similarly to how you started it, with a dip-to-color transition.

Replacing Transitions

Although you could go back into the Quick Transition dialog box to switch the last dissolve to a dip-to-color transition, you can access even more effects through the Effect Palette.

To replace transitions using the Effect Palette:

1. Choose **TOOLS > EFFECT PALETTE** or press **CTRL+8** (Windows) or **COMMAND+8** (Mac). The Effect Palette opens, displaying the list of effects you can apply.

Tip: You can save time managing palettes (as well as screen real estate) by using the Effect Palette tab within the Project window.

2. The left side of the Effect Palette lists effect categories and the right side lists the effects within the selected category. Click the **BLEND** category on the left side of the Effect Palette to show all the effects in that category (see Figure 2.19).

3. Drag the **DIP TO COLOR** effect from the right side of the Effect Palette to the last transition in the Timeline. As shown in Figure 2.20, the transition in the Timeline becomes highlighted when you drag the effect over it. The new effect will replace the old one, but keep the same alignment and duration.

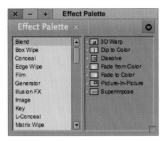

Figure 2.19
The Blend effects.

Figure 2.20
Dragging the effect onto the Timeline.

Tip: Dragging a transition effect onto a cut adds a one-second transition centered on cut.

4. Release the mouse button. The dip-to-color transition replaces the original transition, and a Dip to Color icon appears on the clip. Notice that this icon features a green dot, as do the transitions you applied earlier. This dot indicates that the effect can play in real time. It does not require rendering.

5. Press the **HOME** key to place the position indicator at the start of the project. (If you use a Mac with no Home key, press the **FUNCTION+LEFT ARROW** keyboard shortcut.)

6. Press the **SPACE BAR** to play the sequence. Press it again to stop playback after Matt Damon says, "With people and cultures as unpredictable as the landscape."

Having a dip-to-color transition on both ends works better to encapsulate the short montage. After your effect is applied, positioned, and aligned, you must use Effect mode to further customize it.

Modifying Effects in Effect Mode

In Effect mode, an Effect Editor displays all the parameters you can adjust for any given effect. To select the effect you want to adjust, you first place the position indicator over it and enable the track on which the effect is located. The parameters for that effect will be displayed when you enter Effect mode. Let's modify the dip-to-color transition so that instead of dipping to black, it dips to a more appropriate desert color.

To modify effects in Effect mode:

1. In the Timeline, place the position indicator over the last dip-to-color transition.

2. Make sure the **V1** track is active.

3. To enter Effect mode, click the **EFFECT MODE** button at the bottom of the Composer window, as shown in Figure 2.21. The Effect Editor appears with a list of parameter categories available for the Dip to Color effect. (See Figure 2.22.)

Figure 2.21
The Effect Mode button.

Figure 2.22
The Effect Editor.

Tip: You can also enter Effect mode by choosing Windows > Workspaces > Effect Editing. This workspace reorganizes Media Composer's layout to display the windows you need while in Effect mode.

4. The Effect Editor organizes effect parameters in collapsible groups, with each item representing a way to manipulate an image. The type of the parameters available varies according to the effect you are modifying. Click the triangle next to the **BACKGROUND COLOR** item to open the group and view the parameters, shown in Figure 2.23. The sliders that appear enable you to adjust various color parameters.

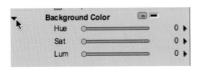

Figure 2.23
The Background Color group.

5. For the background, you can either drag the sliders or use a visual color palette. To open the color palette, click the **OTHER OPTIONS** button in the Background Color group (see Figure 2.24). Depending on your operating system, this opens the Select Color window (Mac) or the Color dialog box (Windows).

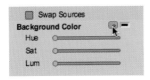

Figure 2.24
The Other Options button.

6. If you're using a Mac, click the **COLOR SLIDERS** drop-down list at the top of the Select Color window and choose **RGB SLIDERS**. Set the **RED** slider to **105**, the **GREEN** slider to **75**, and the **BLUE** slider to **55**, as shown in Figure 2.25. On a Windows PC, type the same values into the **RED**, **GREEN**, and **BLUE** fields. This should produce a nice, dark, sandy-brown color that our transition will dip to and from. When you're finished, click the **OK** button; the picture in the Record monitor changes to a sandy desert color, reflecting the changes you made.

Figure 2.25
Set the desired color.

7. To preview the transition, click the **PLAY LOOP** button on the right side of the Effect Editor (see Figure 2.26); then press the **SPACE BAR** to stop playing the transition.

Figure 2.26
The Play Loop button.

Customizing an effect can produce results that better fit the feeling of your program. But before you leave Effect mode, the next section will teach you how to preserve your customized transition for later use.

Saving Effect Templates

After creating a great effect, you may want to reuse it in other parts of your sequence. For those occasions, you can save effects as templates and use them repeatedly without having to re-create them. Templates are saved in bins, so the first step is to create a bin just for your saved templates.

To save effect templates:

1. With the Bin tab selected in the Project window, click the **NEW BIN** button. Name the new bin **EFFECTS**.

2. If you are not already in Effect mode, place the position indicator over the last dip-to-color transition in the Timeline and click the **EFFECT MODE** button to open the Effect Editor.

3. From the upper-left corner of the Effect Editor, drag the **DIP TO COLOR** icon (see Figure 2.27) into the newly created Effects bin. A new bin item is displayed, named Dip to Color.

Figure 2.27
The Dip to Color icon in the Effect Editor.

4. If you are into waterboarding or electro-shock treatments, you can leave the name as is. Alternatively, you can preserve your mental health and give it a more descriptive name. Click the **Dip to Color** item in the bin and type **Dip to Raw Umber**. That's much more exciting than Dip to Brown! The name alone makes you want to use it again, right?

5. Let's reuse the effect template on the first dip-to-color transition so the start and end of the scenic montage match. From the Effects bin, drag the **Dip to Raw Umber** template onto the first **Dip to Color** icon in the Timeline, as shown in Figure 2.28.

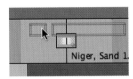

Figure 2.28
Reusing the effect template.

Note: Depending on how much you adjusted the dip-to-color duration in the Timeline, the template may require more handle than what is available when you apply it. Media Composer will display an Insufficient Source dialog box if there is not enough handle. You can choose the Size to Fit option in the dialog box to have Media Composer change the duration of the effect to fit the available handle size.

6. With all the transitions in place and customized to fit the program, let's view the sequence. Close the **Effects** bin.

7. Press the **Home** key to place the position indicator at the start of the project. (If you use a Mac with no Home key, press the **Function+Left Arrow** keyboard shortcut.)

8. Press the **space bar** to play the sequence. Press it again to stop playback after Matt Damon says, "With people and cultures as unpredictable as the landscape."

You'll probably use these transitions more than any other effect in Media Composer. That doesn't mean, however, that other effects won't improve the impact of shots just as much. Next, you'll learn a bit more about other types of effects you can apply in Media Composer.

Adding Segment Effects

In Media Composer, effects can be broken down into three different types:

- **Transition effects.** As you've learned, these are applied at the transition point between two clips, often to emphasize a change of time or theme. Transition effects include dissolves, dip-to-color transitions, wipes, pushes, squeezes, and spins.

- **Segment effects.** These are applied to an entire clip within a sequence to change the look of a clip. Segment effects include color effects, masks, and resizes.

- **Motion effects.** These are applied to entire clips within a sequence or to source clips to vary the frame rate or motion of the footage. Motion effects are covered in more depth later in this book.

Note: No matter which type of effect you want to apply, you can access it from the Effect Palette.

Media Composer offers more than 90 customizable transition and segment effects. All segment effects are accessed through the Effect Palette.

To add segment effects:

1. If the Effect Palette isn't open already, choose **TOOLS > EFFECT PALETTE** or press **CTRL+8** (Windows) or **COMMAND+8** (Mac) to open the Effect Palette.

2. Click the **IMAGE** entry on the left side of the Effect Palette to show all effects in the Image category, as shown in Figure 2.29. The Image category has a number of commonly used segment effects that can be useful in any project.

Figure 2.29
Displaying effects in the Image category.

3. Review the project to find a shot that requires a change. To begin, press the **HOME** key to place the position indicator at the start of the project. (If you use a Mac with no Home key, press the **FUNCTION+LEFT ARROW** keyboard shortcut.)

4. Press the **SPACE BAR** to play the sequence. Press it again to stop playback after Matt Damon says, "With people and cultures as unpredictable as the landscape."

5. The narration plays over a series of people shots, from the Woman with Bag on Head shot to the night shot of people dancing around a pole. During these shots, your eye must dart back and forth across the screen because each shot has its subject framed on opposite sides. It would be less strenuous if your eye could stay in a similar area of the frame for at least two consecutive shots. To make this so, drag the position indicator in the Timeline back and forth over the **BOY ON ROCK** clip (see Figure 2.30) and the **MOTHER WITH BABY** clip, around 17 seconds into the sequence.

Figure 2.30
The Boy on Rock clip.

6. Moving the boy to the other side of the frame would align it better with the mother and baby. To enact this, drag the **FLOP** icon from the right side of the Effect Palette to the **BOY ON ROCK** segment in the Timeline. As shown in Figure 2.31, the segment becomes highlighted.

Figure 2.31
Dragging the Flop effect to the Boy on Rock segment.

7. Release the mouse button. The effect is applied, and the Flop icon appears on the clip.

Tip: If you apply an effect to a segment or transition that already has an effect, the new effect replaces the old one.

8. Let's review the segment effect. Press the **HOME** key to place the position indicator at the start of the project. (If you use a Mac with no Home key, press the **FUNCTION+LEFT ARROW** keyboard shortcut.)

9. Press the SPACE BAR to play the sequence. Press it again to stop playback after Matt Damon says, "With people and cultures as unpredictable as the landscape."

Adding an Effect to Multiple Segments

If you have more than one segment that requires the same effect, you can easily do that using the Effect Palette. The first flop effect worked so well, let's add it to two more segments.

To add an effect to multiple segments:

1. Click the SEGMENT MODE button in the Smart Tool palette, as shown in Figure 2.32.

Figure 2.32
The Segment Mode button.

Tip: You can use either Segment tool in the Smart Tool palette to select segments for adding effects.

2. To add the flop effect to the Woman with Bag on Head and B-Roll 01 clips, you must first select them both. Click the WOMAN WITH BAG ON HEAD segment; then, while pressing the SHIFT key, click the B-ROLL 01 segment to select them both. As shown in Figure 2.33, both segments become highlighted in the Timeline.

Figure 2.33
Selecting multiple segments.

Tip: If you accidentally select the wrong segment, click it again to deselect it.

3. Double-click the FLOP entry on the right side of the Effect Palette. The flop effect is applied to both segments in the Timeline.

4. Click the **Segment** tool in the Smart Tool palette to disable it.

5. Drag the position indicator just before the **Woman with Bag on Head** segment and play the sequence to view the newly added effects.

Well, this proves you can have too much of a good thing. Not all of these flops work well when you view them back to back. Fortunately, Media Composer does make it easy to try different combinations of effects. If they don't work out (like in this case), it's just as easy to remove them.

Removing Segment Effects

Similar to removing transitions, the Remove Effect button can also be used to remove segment effects.

To remove segment effects:

1. Make sure the **V1** track is still selected in the Track Selector panel.

2. Place the position indicator directly over the last clip with the flop applied (the B-Roll, 01 segment). This is one segment where the unflopped shot worked better to draw your eye across the frame.

3. Click the **Remove Effect** button (see Figure 2.34) or press **Shift+** (**backslash**). The flop is removed and the man switches back to being on the right side of the frame (see Figure 2.35).

Figure 2.34
The Remove Effect button.

Figure 2.35
Unflopping the shot.

4. Watch the sequence in its entirety to see all your changes. To begin, press the **HOME** key to place the position indicator at the start of the project. (If you use a Mac with no Home key, press the **FUNCTION+LEFT ARROW** keyboard shortcut.)

5. Press the **SPACE BAR** to play the sequence all the way through to the end.

All these effects really work together to enhance the sequence. They create the perfect mood for this trailer. You should now have a good understanding of how to apply and modify both transition and segment effects and how effects can change the pace of the sequence as well as set a tone. In the next project, you'll apply effects not to set a mood but to correct problems that occurred during production.

Review/Discussion Questions

1. Where is the Quick Transition button and what is its default keyboard shortcut?

2. If you want to add multiple dissolves to a series of cut points in the Timeline, how do you identify the cuts that will get the dissolves?

3. What are the three types of effects, and how are they different?

4. What is handle, and why is it important?

5. What must you do to ensure a Quick Transition is added only to a video cut point, and not an audio cut point?

6. True or false: The Transition Corner display shows the first, middle, and last frames of the A and B sides of the transition.

7. True or false: Dragging a transition from the Effect Palette onto an existing transition in the Timeline replaces the existing transition.

8. True or false: To save a template, you drag the effect icon from the upper-left corner of the Effect Editor into the Effect Palette.

9. What button must be clicked before dragging a transition in the Timeline in order to change its duration or position?

10. When you want to add a segment effect to multiple segments, what button do you use to select the segments?

Lesson 2 Keyboard Shortcuts

Key	Shortcut
\ (backslash)	Open the Quick Transition dialog box
Shift+\ (backslash)	Remove the effect under the position indicator
Ctrl+8 (Windows)/Command+8 (Mac)	Open the Effect Palette

Applying Transition Effects

With the rough cut finished, you can further polish the documentary segment by adding and modifying some basic effects.

Media Used:
Running the Sahara

Duration:
15 minutes

GOALS

- Apply transition effects
- Change the duration of a transition effect

1. Continuing with the **RTS FX PT2 LESSON 02** sequence that you have been working on, apply 24-frame dissolves to the three cuts that happen between 20:00 and 24:00 in the sequence. Do this by opening the Quick Transition dialog box only once.

2. Modify the first dissolve of the three that you added by making it a 12-frame dissolve that starts at the transition. Do this using the Quick Transition dialog box.

3. Remove the middle dissolve from the three that were just added.

4. For the last dissolve, modify the duration to be 1:12 and have two-thirds of the dissolve happen before the transition and the remaining third happen after it. Make these changes by dragging and positioning the effect in the Timeline.

Corrective Effects

When we talk about visual effects, we often think about spectacular spaceships, wand-wielding wizards, and the always-popular flesh-eating demon. Those are fantastic visual effects, but more often, effects are used to correct shots that have problems. These "hidden" effects are used to remove unwanted elements, smooth out a shaky shot, or subtly warp jump cuts into one seamless shot. As an editor, you will probably be called on to create these corrective effects more often than to create a flesh-eating demon. In this lesson, we'll cover a few of the common tools used to improve a variety of imperfect shots.

Media Used: Running the Sahara

Duration: 60 minutes

GOALS

- Resize clips
- Use Stabilize techniques
- Track blurs and mosaics
- Remove wires or scratches
- Hide jump cuts with Fluid Morph

Resizing a Shot in the Effect Preview Monitor

If you've used a crop tool to cut out unwanted scenery around the edges of a photo, you'll understand the value of resizing clips in Media Composer. The difference is that instead of cropping down a photo, you scale up a clip to fill the monitor and focus on a specific area. The result is the same: Unwanted material around the edges of a shot can be removed, focusing the attention of the viewer on the important area.

To use the Media Composer Crop tool:

1. Launch Media composer, select the **RUNNING THE SAHARA** project on the left side of the Open Project dialog box, and then click **OPEN**. The Project window opens and lists all the bins associated with this project.

2. Double-click the **RTS PT2 FX SEQUENCES** bin in the Project window.

3. In the bin that opens, double-click the **RTS FX PT2 LESSON 03** sequence. The sequence appears in the Record monitor, as shown in Figure 3.1. This is a different section of the Running the Sahara trailer you were working with earlier in this book.

Figure 3.1
Viewing the RTS FX PT2 Lesson 03 in the Record monitor.

4. Whenever you begin working on a project, you should always view it to know what you are dealing with, so that's how you'll start this exercise. Place the position indicator at the start of the project by pressing the **HOME** key on the keyboard. (If you are on a Mac without a Home key, press the **FUNCTION+LEFT ARROW** keyboard shortcut.)

5. Press the **SPACE BAR** to play the project until the end. As you view the sequence, you'll see that there are a number of problems in this section of the trailer that could benefit from some corrective visual effects work. The problems are already identified using markers.

6. Choose **TOOLS** > **MARKERS** to open the Markers window shown in Figure 3.2. Each marker in the Markers window represents a location in the sequence that needs work. You can use the Markers window to jump directly to each segment you'll work on.

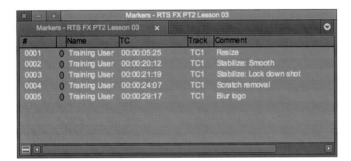

Figure 3.2
The Markers window contains markers for each segment you'll fix.

7. In the Markers window, double-click the first marker, which has the comment "Resize." The position indicator jumps to the marker's location in the Timeline. The shot, of one of the runners and another man greeting each other (see Figure 3.3), has a slight problem. Let's first play it and then discuss how to fix it.

Figure 3.3
Use the Resize effect on this clip to focus the viewer's attention.

8. Make sure only the **V1** track is highlighted, and then press **T** to mark the clip.

9. Click the **PLAY IN TO OUT** button under the Record monitor or press **6** on the keyboard. As the clip plays, the focus of the viewer should be on the runner, but you just can't help being drawn away by the woman turning and looking into the camera. To focus the audience on the runner and avoid paying royalties to the woman on the right, you'll use the Resize effect to scale the image up until she is out of the picture.

10. Choose **TOOLS > EFFECT PALETTE** or press **COMMAND+8** (Mac) or **ALT+8** (Windows).

11. In the Effect Palette, select the **IMAGE** category and drag the **RESIZE** effect onto the highlighted segment in the Timeline, which you just played. Next, you'll make changes to the Resize effect using Effect mode.

12. Click the **EFFECT MODE** button (shown in Figure 3.4) or choose **TOOLS > EFFECT EDITOR**. The Effect Editor opens with the Resize parameters displayed. When you enter Effect mode, the Record monitor becomes the Effect Preview monitor and the position bar under the Effect Preview monitor no longer represents the entire sequence but only the selected segment. In the Effect Preview monitor you can reduce the size of the frame, making it easier to work outside the boundaries of the image.

Figure 3.4
The Effect Mode button is used to open the Effect Editor and enter Effect mode.

13. Click the **REDUCE** button under the Effect Preview monitor (see Figure 3.5). The frame is now 75% of its size. A white outline surrounds the frame. This outline allows you to directly manipulate the Resize effect in the Effect Preview monitor. But before you resize the image, it can be helpful to open the Scaling parameter group in the Effect Editor so you can see the scale values as you change them.

Figure 3.5
Use the Reduce button to zoom out on the Effect Preview monitor.

14. In the Effect Editor, click the disclosure triangle for the **SCALING** parameter group. Now, as you make changes in the Effect Preview monitor you'll be able to see their accurate values. For resizing, changes can be made by dragging the white handles on the frame outline. The handle in the upper right is used to maintain the aspect ratio.

15. In the Effect Preview monitor, drag the upper-right handle out to the right until the X and Y Scaling values in the Effect Editor are set to 125, as shown in Figure 3.6. When you release the mouse, the image is scaled from the center but the woman is still slightly in the frame. You can reposition the scaled image over to the right to eliminate the remaining part of the woman that is still in the frame.

Figure 3.6
Use the handles to resize the image in the Effect Preview monitor.

16. Click anywhere within the white outline and drag it so the outline's upper-left corner is flush with the upper-left corner of the frame, as shown in Figure 3.7.

Figure 3.7
The result of the Resize effect eliminates unwanted material around the edges.

17. Below the Effect Preview monitor click the **PLAY IN TO OUT** button or press the **6** key to see the results of the Resize effect play back in the monitor.

18. Click the **ENLARGE** button to scale the frame back up. Then close the Effect Editor to return to Source/Record mode.

You've successfully refocused the audience's attention onto the runner and, in doing so, made the credits to the movie shorter by removing the unwanted cast member.

Smoothing Shaky Camera Movement

Another common problem you are sure to encounter as an editor is unstable camera work. In a documentary, it's not always possible to be on a tripod; and sometimes that slowly roaming camera work is desirable, but you just want it toned down. Media Composer has a flexible stabilization effect that can either lock an unstable shot down, removing all movement, or eliminate any erratic bumps and jitters but keep the general camera movement. The beauty of this effect is that it is almost totally automatic.

To fix an unstable shot:

1. From the Markers window, double-click the second marker, with the comment "Stabilize: Smooth" (see Figure 3.8). After you double-click the marker, the position indicator jumps to the marker's location in the Timeline. Let's play before adding any effects.

Figure 3.8
The second marker identifies a clip that needs to be smoothed.

2. Make sure only the **V1** track is highlighted then press **T** to mark the clip.

3. Click the **PLAY IN TO OUT** button under the Record monitor or press **6** on the keyboard. This shot, shown in Figure 3.8, has a little camera move going on, which gives it that nice documentary feel, but there are a few bumps that make it jarring. The Stabilize effect begins working immediately after you apply it to a segment in the Timeline. It analyzes the clip frame by frame in order to extract motion data. Then it inverts the motion data and applies it to the clip. Then, when the camera moves down to the left, the motion data offsets it by repositioning the frame up to the right. The result is a clip that appears static because it moves in opposite directions by the same amount.

Note: Media Composer includes three effects that can stabilize a shot:

   ■ **Stabilize.** In general, the Stabilize effect should be your first choice. It is the most flexible choice and usually does a good job automatically. If necessary, you can also try it in Manual mode to take more control over the process.

   ■ **Regional Stabilize.** This effect is "old school." It does not have an automatic mode, so it's up to you to select a region to stabilize. It is also not a real-time effect, so it must be rendered. It does, however, provide a Progressive Source option, so you can use it on progressive material in an interlaced project.

   ■ **3D Warp.** The 3D Warp effect has the Stabilize effect built into it, so you can stabilize a segment with all the other features included in the 3D Warp feature. Nice, but overkill if you just need to stabilize a shot.

4. From the Effect Palette, drag the **STABILIZE** effect, shown in Figure 3.9, onto the highlighted clip in the Timeline. Almost immediately after you apply the effect, the Tracking window opens, and tracking points appear in the Effect Preview monitor as the clip steps forward frame by frame. You can review the results by playing the clip.

Figure 3.9
The Stabilize effect is found in the Image category of the Effect Palette.

5. Click **PLAY IN TO OUT** under the Effect Preview monitor or press the
   6 key. The Effect Editor includes blue highlighted enable buttons
   for active parameters. You can disable the Stabilize effect by disabling
   the active parameters in the Effect Editor.

6. In the Effect Editor, click the enable buttons for **SCALING** and **POSITION**, as
   shown in Figure 3.10. Disabling parameter groups in the Effect Editor is
   a good way to compare the results with the original video. The parameter
   group's settings are still retained, so they can be enabled again at any time.

Figure 3.10
Disable Effect Editor parameters to compare
the shot with and without the effect.

7. Click **PLAY IN TO OUT** under the Effect Preview monitor or press the **6**
   key to play the segment without the Stabilize effect enabled.

8. In the Effect Editor, click the enable buttons for **SCALING** and **POSITION** to
   reapply the Stabilize results. Then close the Effect Editor.

The result is a smoother camera move that still retains the overall documentary feel.
That is just one method to apply the Stabilize effect. You can also use it to lock
down a shot to completely remove the camera movement. In the next section, you'll
learn how to modify some of the Tracking window options to get a lockdown result.

Locking Down Shaky Camera Movement

Another stabilization technique aims to create a locked-down shot. All camera
movement is removed, and the clip appears as if the camera were on a tripod. The
same Stabilize effect is used, but instead of letting it perform an automatic stabilization, you intervene and set some parameters.

To create a locked-down shot:

1. From the Markers window, double-click the third marker with the comment
   "Stabilize: Lock Down Shot." Again, the position indicator jumps to the
   marker's location in the Timeline, ready to play the clip before adding any
   effects.

2. Make sure only the **V1** track is highlighted; then press **T** to mark the clip, as shown in Figure 3.11.

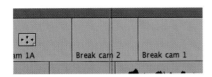

Figure 3.11
Mark the clip.

3. Click the **PLAY IN TO OUT** button under the Record monitor or press **6** on the keyboard. This is a short clip that would look better locked down than moving around, considering its duration. You'll use the same Stabilize effect but cancel automatic stabilization to create a locked-down result.

4. From the Effect Palette, drag the **STABILIZE** effect onto the highlighted clip in the Timeline. When the Tracking window appears (see Figure 3.12), press the **SPACE BAR** to stop the automatic tracking process that begins. The Tracking window that opens when you apply the Stabilize effect is where you can select a different tracking engine, add tracking data points, and enable or disable the Steady Glide option, which smoothes the camera movement. Although you could use the same Fluid Stabilizer that you used in the previous section, you'll choose a new engine to learn the difference.

Figure 3.12
The Tracking window is used to select a tracking engine and other tracking options.

5. In the Tracking window, choose the **CORRELATION TRACKER** from the pop-up menu.

6. To lock down the stabilization and not just smooth the camera move, disable the **STEADY GLIDE** option, shown in Figure 3.13.

Figure 3.13
Disabling the Steady Glide option creates a locked-down shot.

Note: Stabilization is based on the ability to track regions of an image over a number of frames. Tracking creates motion data that can be used to stabilize a clip or to match the movement from one shot in order to composite another shot or object on top. In either case, Media Composer includes three different tracking engines you can choose from when stabilizing or match moving:

- **Fluid Stabilizer.** This is the primary tracking engine. This engine automatically analyzes multiple tracking regions in an image over a number of frames to create motion data. It is best used for smoothing jittery camera movement, and it should be your first choice in most cases.

- **Correlation Tracker.** This is a more traditional tracking engine. After you select a high-contrast region, the Correlation Tracker will follow it frame by frame to create the motion data used to stabilize. The benefit is that it is fast and accurate as long as you have a well-defined, high-contrast region to track throughout the entire clip.

- **Fluid Tracker.** This is used in very specific situations involving corner pinning or tracking objects that start outside the visible frame. It may be faster than the Correlation Tracker if the region you are trying to track is a large area of the frame.

7. From the **DISPLAY** pop-up menu, choose **TRACKING DATA** to see the tracking data points and path.

8. In the Tracking window Timeline, drag the position indicator all the way to the left, to the first frame of the clip, as shown in Figure 3.14.

Figure 3.14
Move the Tracking window Timeline
position indicator to the first frame.

The yellow tracking data point is now displayed in the Effect Preview monitor. Ideally, you position the tracking data point over a well-defined, high-contrast region of the image that remains onscreen and unobstructed for the duration of the segment. In this shot, the sand and sky are not good selections because there is almost no detail. The man's face might work, but the features of his face move as he speaks, which will add a secondary motion that you don't want in the stabilization. His ear is probably a good first choice. It is high contrast against the sky, and it doesn't move as he speaks.

Tip: When using the Correlation Tracker, only one tracking data point is required if the camera is moving up, down, and side to side. If the camera is also rotating or zooming, then an additional tracking data point is required.

9. In the Effect Preview monitor, drag the tracking data point so it is placed over the top of the man's ear, as shown in Figure 3.15.

Figure 3.15
Place the tracking data point over the top of the ear.

10. In the Tracking window, click the **START TRACKING** button to begin tracking, as shown in Figure 3.16. Very quickly the segment moves forward frame-by-frame in the Effect Preview monitor. For every frame advance, the tracking data point searches within the outer yellow search rectangle to locate the same region you initially selected. When the tracking is complete, a yellow tracking path will appear in the Effect Preview monitor, which indicates how the camera moves during the segment.

Figure 3.16
Click the Start Tracking button to being tracking.

Tip: On fast-moving shots, it's very possible that the region you select will fall outside the outer yellow search rectangle as the frame advances. In that case, you can resize the outer search rectangle to increase the search size and try retracking. Increasing the search size will also increase the time it takes to complete the track.

11. To see the stabilization results, choose **EFFECT RESULTS** from the **DISPLAY** pop-up menu and press the **6** key on the keyboard to play IN to OUT. Then close the Tracking window and the Effect Editor.

The segment no longer has any camera movement. In some cases, you may want to try a new point to see if you can get better results. Just select Tracking Data in the Display pop-up menu, place the position indicator at the start of the Tracking window Timeline, reposition the tracking data point, and click Start track.

Tracking and Blurring Unwanted Objects

Stabilization is one of the uses for tracking data. The other use is to match the camera movement in a segment in order to composite an image or graphic on top of the segment. Media Composer not only allows you to use a tracker for those situations, but it also includes a tracker built in to some very useful image-processing effects. One of the most common is a Blur effect, which allows you to blur out a face or logo even if the face or logo is moving.

To track and blur unwanted objects:

1. From the Markers window, double-click the last marker, with the comment "Blur Logo." Again, the position indicator jumps to the marker's location in the Timeline, ready to play the clip shown in Figure 3.17, before adding any effects.

Figure 3.17
The last marker identifies a segment with an unwanted logo.

2. Make sure only the **V1** track is highlighted and then press **T** to mark the clip.

3. Click the **PLAY IN TO OUT** button under the Record monitor or press **6** on the keyboard. This shot has a big logo on the goggles the runner is wearing. Product placement is big business, and this company is not one of the sponsors, so you can't let this go by. One way to correct this shot is to blur out the logo. Obviously you want the blur to be as unobtrusive as possible, but the logo moves so much that only a large blur would cover the entire area of the frame. Luckily, Media Composer includes a Blur effect with a built-in tracker.

4. From the Effect Palette's **IMAGE** category, drag the **BLUR** effect onto the highlighted segment in the Timeline and then click the **EFFECT MODE** button to open the Effect Editor. The Blur effect does nothing to the image by default. The first step is to track the area you want to blur out.

5. To open the Tracking window, click the **TRACKING** button on the side of the Effect Editor, as shown in Figure 3.18.

Figure 3.18
In the Effect Editor, the Tracking button opens the Tracking window.

6. Drag the position bar in the Tracking window Timeline to the start of the segment.

7. In the Effect Preview monitor, drag the tracking data point to the blue corner rim of the goggles, as shown in Figure 3.19.

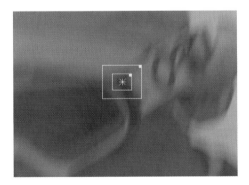

Figure 3.19
Position the tracking data point on the corner of the goggles.

8. Click the **START TRACKING** button in the Tracking window. As the Effect Preview monitor moves forward frame by frame, you'll notice that the tracking data point loses the region you selected for it. The logo bounces and moves too far across the screen as the man runs for the tracker to locate it.

You can correct this by increasing the size of the outer yellow search rectangle. This increases the area where the tracker will look for the tracking data point as it moves forward frame by frame.

9. Drag the position bar in the Tracking window Timeline to the start of the segment.

10. In the Effect Preview monitor, drag the upper-right corner of the outer search rectangle up as far as it will go to increase the search region. Drag it out to the right until it makes a perfect square, as shown in Figure 3.20. Now you have a very large search region for the tracker to look in to locate the blue rim of the goggles. If the runner wasn't bobbing up and down as much, the search region could be smaller, but in this case we need a fairly large search region.

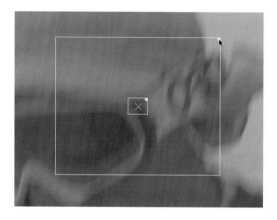

Figure 3.20
Increasing the search area is useful when tracking fast-moving objects.

11. Click the **START TRACKING** button in the Tracking window. Increasing the search region's size improved the tracking immensely. You now have a good track for the blur to attach to. This particular Blur effect (along with the Mosaic effect) in the Image category fills in a shape drawn by the editor to blur the offensive area. The next step is to draw a shape around the logo to blur it out.

12. Drag the position bar under the Effect preview monitor to the first frame of the segment, as shown in Figure 3.21.

Figure 3.21
The Effect Preview monitor's position bar is for the segment, the not the entire sequence.

13. Select the **RECTANGLE** tool on the side of the Effect Editor.

14. Draw a rectangle over the blue logo in the Effect Preview monitor, as shown in Figure 3.22. The rectangle appears in the Effect Preview monitor filled with a Blur effect that covers the blue logo. To make sure it moves along the tracking path, you must enable the tracker in the Effect Editor.

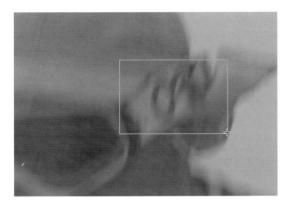

Figure 3.22
Use the Rectangle tool to draw over the logo in the Effect Preview monitor.

15. In the Effect Editor, click the **TRACKING** group's disclosure triangle to view the tracking parameters.

16. In the tracking parameters, click the enable button for the first tracker, labeled **NO TRACKER**. Enabling this tracker automatically assigns the tracking data point you created in the Tracking window to the Blur effect's shape. If you had used more than one tracking data point, you could select it from the menu in the Effect Editor shown in Figure 3.23.

Figure 3.23
Enabling a tracker assigns the tracking data point to the Blur effect's shape.

17. Press **6** to play IN to OUT and view the effect's results in the Effect Preview monitor.

The Blur effect works well to block out the logo while not being too obtrusive in the shot. Even though the shape is drawn and attached to the tracker, you can still modify the blur amount or even the shape itself using the parameters and tools in the Effect Editor. The modification can even vary over the duration of the segment, which you'll see in the next section.

Using Standard Keyframes

When you played the Blur effect, you may have noticed that the runner turns his head, revealing more of the logo toward the end of the shot. The blurred square remains the same size throughout the segment, so even though it tracks to the correct location, it is too small to hide the entire logo by the end. To solve this type of problem, Media Composer allows you to modify parameters (including the shape) over time using a technique called *keyframing*. You'll learn more about advanced keyframing in a later lesson, but in this lesson we'll use the standard keyframing built into the Effect Preview monitor.

This section picks up where the last one left off, so you should still be on the clip from the last marker, in Effect mode, with the added Blur effect. Under the Effect Preview monitor is a position bar that represents the duration of the segment. Pink triangles located at the start and end of the position bar are called *keyframes*, which are placed there by default on almost all effects. By selecting the first keyframe, any parameter changes you make are set for only the first frame. Selecting the last keyframe and changing parameters sets the parameter values for only the last frame. Media Composer will then interpolate between the different parameter values to create a smooth animation. You'll use keyframes to change the shape used for the blur so that it better covers the logo throughout the segment. The shape on the first keyframe is good, so you just need to change the shape on the last keyframe

To use keyframing:

1. In the Effect Preview monitor, select the last keyframe on the far right of the position bar, as shown in Figure 3.24. When you select the last keyframe, the position bar moves to the last frame of the effect, but more importantly, the first keyframe is deselected. Now, using the Reshape tool in the Effect Editor, you can change the shape of the blur to better cover the logo.

Figure 3.24
Triangular keyframes are placed at the start and end of the position bar.

2. Select the **RESHAPE** tool on the side of the Effect Editor as shown in Figure 3.25; then, in the Effect Preview monitor, drag each of the four corners of the Blur shape to best cover the logo, as shown in Figure 3.26.

Figure 3.25
Select the Reshape tool to correct the blur rectangle.

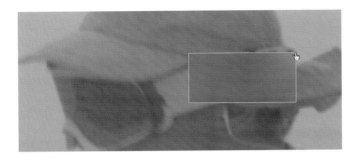

Figure 3.26
Reshape the rectangle in the Effect
Preview monitor to cover the logo.

3. To see how the shape changes from the start of the effect to the end, drag the position bar backward to the start of the segment. To make it easier to know where you are within an effect, the top right of the Effect Preview monitor displays the duration of the effect and the current time within the effect.

4. Using the effect time display, drag the position indicator in the position bar to **1:00** (00:00:29:24 on Master timecode).

Tip: Dragging the position indicator in the Timeline will cause you to exit Effect mode. Use the position bar to move the position indicator within the effect and stay in Effect mode.

The interpolation between the first and last keyframe doesn't perfectly match the runner's head turn, so some of the logo appears in this frame. You can add additional keyframes anywhere within the position bar just by changing the shape.

5. In the Effect Preview monitor, drag the top-right and bottom-right corners of the blur shape to best cover the logo, as shown in Figure 3.27. A keyframe is automatically added at the current time.

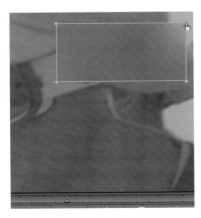

Figure 3.27
A keyframe is added in the Effect Preview
monitor when you drag the rectangle.

6. Using the effect time display, drag the position indicator in the position bar to **:23** (00:00:29:17 on Master timecode). At this frame, the runner's head has not yet turned, so the logo appears much smaller. You no longer need such a big shape, so you can correct the shape on the current frame to automatically create a keyframe.

7. In the Effect Preview monitor, drag the top-right and bottom-right corners of the blur shape to the left to best cover the logo.

8. To see how the shape changes from the start of the effect to the end with the newly added keyframes, drag the position bar backward to the start of the segment.

9. Press the **6** key to play the effect from IN to OUT and review the blur in real time.

Nicely done. You successfully tracked and blurred the logo. You could further refine the blur using feathering in the Effect Editor, but if you want it to be applied across the entire effect, you must now be sure to select all the keyframes in the position bar before making the parameter change.

Hiding Jump Cuts with Fluid Morph

Although most corrective effects are segment effects, Media Composer does have a unique transition effect that can also be used to hide problems in a sequence. Fluid Morph specifically helps solve the problem of jump cuts, where two shots of the same subject are edited back to back with only slight differences between them. It's a jarring cut because elements within the frame suddenly pop on screen in a different place. Fluid Morph is able to warp the two images to better align with each other, so they perform a more seamless transition. For this exercise, you'll return to the sequence from Lesson 2, "Introduction to Visual Effects," to improve a jump cut that happens during one of the interviews.

To hide jump cuts:

1. In the RTS PT2 FX Sequences bin, double-click the **RTS FX Lesson 02** sequence.

2. Choose **Tools > Markers** to open the Markers window if it isn't already open.

3. In the Markers window, double-click the marker with the comment "Jump Cut." The position indicator jumps to the marker's location in the Timeline, as shown in Figure 3.28. This is the cut point between two interview shots. Let's play over the two cuts to see the jump cut problem.

Figure 3.28
The marker identifies the jump cut in the sequence.

4. Make sure only the **V1** track is highlighted.

5. Click the **REWIND** button under the Record monitor to go to the start of the first clip of the transition, as shown in Figure 3.29, and then press **I** to mark an IN point.

Figure 3.29
Mark an IN point at the start of the first clip of the transition.

6. Click the **FAST FORWARD** button twice and then click the **STEP BACKWARD 1 FRAME** button to go to the end of the second clip of the transition, as shown in Figure 3.30. Then press **O** to mark an OUT point.

7. Press **6** on the keyboard to play the jump cut that happens between the IN and OUT marks. At the end of the sentence "it's never been done," the man's head pops to a different place on the screen. Everything else is exactly the same, making this a perfect candidate for a Fluid Morph. Fluid Morph works best when the majority of the image is the same and the difference in the object that moves is not too severe.

Figure 3.30
Mark an OUT point at the
end of the second clip of
the transition.

8. In the Effect Palette, select the **ILLUSION FX** category, as shown in Figure
    3.31, and then drag the **FLUID MORPH** effect onto the highlighted jump
    cut transition. You may recall from Lesson 2 that the default duration for
    a transition is 1:00. That's much too long for a Fluid Morph, so you'll first
    change the duration to something shorter.

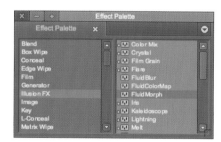

Figure 3.31
Fluid Morph is located in the Illusion
FX category of the Effect Palette.

9. Click the **EFFECT MODE** button to open the Effect Editor.

10. At the bottom of the Effect Editor, type **10** into the **DURATION** field to
    create a 10-frame Fluid Morph transition, as shown in Figure 3.32.

Figure 3.32
The duration of a transition can be entered in the Effect Editor.

The Fluid Morph does not require any user input to work, although there
are a few options in the Effect Editor. Before you try the options, let's step
through the effect in the Effect Preview monitor to see the default results.

Since the Fluid Morph is not a real-time effect, you must click through the position bar at the bottom of the Effect Preview monitor to view the results and not drag through it.

11. Click at the start of the Effect Preview monitor's position bar on the far left to see the first frame of the effect; then click on the hash marks going left to right in the position bar to see the various stages of the effect. Although the effect looks good when you click through the position bar, the subtlety of this effect can really be judged only by playing it, which requires rendering.

12. Click the **RENDER EFFECT** button at the bottom of the Effect Editor.

13. In the Render Effect dialog box, select the hard drive where you want the effect media to be stored, then click **OK**.

14. Since the effect is only 10 frames long, playing the transition in Effect mode will be too short to evaluate it accurately. You'll play this effect using the IN to OUT marks in the Timeline in order to get more context surrounding the transition. In the Timeline, click the mark IN point.

15. Press the **6** key to play IN to OUT.

This morph looks really good. In cases where you might need a bit more help, there are a few options in the Effect Editor. Feature Match should be your first choice. By default, Fluid Morph warps both images based on the luminance of the images. Feature Match improves the warping by aligning feature patterns as it warps both images. In this case we didn't need Feature Match, but you will often find better results with that option enabled. The Source menu is the next level of assistance for misaligned Fluid Morphs. By default the Fluid Morph warps each side of the transition frame by frame. This is set as Stream > Stream in the Source menu. Although this is the optimal way to get a natural result, it is also more likely to have artifacts because you have two images moving that must be aligned. Setting one side or the other of the transition at Still instead of Stream might provide fewer artifacts because the Fluid Morph will use a freeze frame in place of moving video during the morph for the side of the transition chosen.

Review/Discussion Questions

1. On a Resize effect, how can you scale a clip in the Effect Preview monitor but maintain the aspect ratio?

2. Where is the position bar and what is it used for?

3. Once a clip is stabilized, how can you compare the stabilized result with the original video?

4. Why would you choose to increase the size of the yellow search rectangle when tracking?

5. When using the Blur effect from the Image category, how do you attach a tracker to the blur shape?

6. What do the Enlarge and Reduce buttons do in the Effect Preview monitor?

7. Under what category is the Fluid Morph located in the Effect Palette?

Lesson 3 Keyboard Shortcuts

Key	Shortcut
Ctrl+8 (Windows)/Command+8 (Mac)	Open Effect Palette

Tracking with the Mosaic Effect

Use your new-found skills with corrective effects to improve two segments from a sequence you have been working on.

Media Used:
Running the Sahara

Duration:
10 minutes

GOALS

- Obscure a license plate by tracking a Mosaic effect over it
- Resize a clip to eliminate distracting cars

1. Return to the **RTS FX PT2 Lesson 03** sequence that you were working on earlier.

2. The clip of the runners at 31:15 has a car in the distance on the right side of the frame and a car on the left that comes into frame at the end of the shot. Use the Resize effect to crop out both the car on the right and the car that comes into the frame on the left.

3. Use the Mosaic effect from the Image category to track a small Mosaic over the motorcycle license plate at 32:00. This effect works similarly to the Blur effect you placed over the logo.

Retiming

When putting a scene together, sometimes the original timing of the shot needs to be adjusted. For example, you may want an exterior shot to last longer than what was actually shot. This chapter introduces you to Motion effects that allow you to vary the playback speed of a clip or freeze the clip entirely.

Media Used: Running the Sahara

Duration: 45 minutes

GOALS

- Explore the different types of Motion effects
- Create a freeze frame
- Create a Motion effect
- Use Fit to Fill to create a Motion effect
- Use a Timewarp preset
- Use a Timewarp as a corrective effect

Types of Motion Effects

Motion effects vary the speed at which frames from clips play. Avid editing systems can create three different types of Motion effects:

- **Freeze frames.** These are applied to a master clip or subclip in the Source monitor and create a new clip containing only the desired frame.

- **Motion effects.** These are also applied to a master clip or subclip in the Source monitor. The rate of motion cannot be varied over time.

- **Timewarp effects.** These are applied to a segment in the Timeline. The rate of motion can be keyframed and varied over time within a single clip.

The key difference between the three different types is that two of them—freeze frames and Motion effects—are created from the source side of the Composer window, while Timewarps are created from footage that already exists in your Timeline. Depending on the stage of your edit, one may be more convenient than the others.

Creating Freeze Frames

A freeze frame displays a single frame from a clip on the screen for a duration you choose. As with Motion effects, these effects are generated from the Source monitor and treated as a new source to be edited into your sequence.

To get started:

1. If the Running the Sahara project is not open from the last lesson, open Media Composer, select the **Running the Sahara** project on the left side of the Open Project dialog box, and click the **Open** button.

2. The Project window opens and lists all the bins associated with this project. The bin you'll use in this lesson is the RTS PT2 FX Sequences bin, which contains a number of sequences you'll use throughout this book. Double-click the **RTS PT2 FX Sequences** bin in the Project window to open it.

3. We'd like to create a freeze frame of a clip already edited into the sequence, and fortunately that's very easy to do. In the RTS PT2 FX Sequences bin window, double-click the **RTS FX PT2 Lesson 04** sequence. The sequence appears in the Record monitor.

Let's move to the correct area of the Timeline from which we wish to generate our freeze frame. To help you quickly jump to the right location, we have set a marker for you.

To move to the desired location in the Timeline:

1. Choose TOOLS > MARKERS to open the Markers window.

2. Double-click the marker named FREEZE FRAME to jump to that location in the Timeline. We'd like to replace the clip at this point with a freeze frame.

To locate the shot you want to use for the freeze frame:

1. From the Project window, open the 2 RTS SOURCE CLIPS bin.

2. Double-click the MINARET clip to load it into the Source monitor. The frame we wish to use is marked with a marker.

3. Click the marker in the Source monitor to jump to the correct frame.

Setting the Freeze Frame Render Type

Because the clip from which we are generating the freeze frame is from a full-resolution clip, we must tell Media Composer how we want it generated. The system can generate freeze frames using three different rendering techniques.

- **Duplicated Field.** The default choice, but not recommended. This option reduces the vertical resolution by half because it drops one field of the image, resulting in a lower-quality image.

- **Both Fields.** Uses both fields. Good for shots without interfield motion or progressive media. Shots with interfield motion will show noticeable jitter due to the temporal differences between the two fields.

- **Interpolated Field.** Good for shots with interfield motion because it deletes field 2 and uses adjacent field 1 to calculate new field 2 data.

You should follow these general rules when selecting the render type:

- Use Interpolated Field when working with NTSC 29.97i, PAL 25i, or 1080i media.

- Use Both Fields when working with NTSC 24p/23.976p, PAL 25p/24p, 720p, or 1080p media.

Tip: Although using Interpolated Field with progressive media will not necessarily get you into trouble—but could result in a slightly softer image—using Both Fields in an interlaced project will almost always get you into trouble due to interfield motion that is present (if not noticeable) prior to creating the freeze frame. A good example of this is the blinking of an eye. A blink will appear as a visible flutter in a freeze frame created from interlaced media using Both Fields.

Understanding Fields and Frames

Back when television was being invented, the goal was to draw the entire picture, one line at a time, from top to bottom. Unfortunately, the technology of the time wouldn't allow that quickly enough to prevent unacceptable motion artifacts. So what they did instead was to draw half of the frame at once, skipping every other line, then draw the second half of the frame, filling in the skipped lines. This is known as *interlacing*, as the frame is made of two interwoven— or interlaced—parts. These two parts are known as *fields*. Figure 4.1 shows the interlacing order for high definition video, with the fields numbered. (Even though interlacing could have been bypassed when high-definition video was created, it was kept for backward compatibility.)

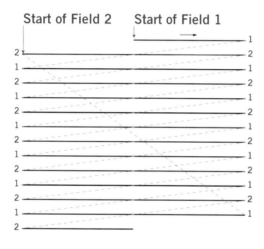

Figure 4.1
Field ordering for 1080i HD video.

The NTSC, PAL, and 1080-line interlaced (often written as 1080i) formats use interlaced fields. 720-line HD is always progressive, and there are progressive versions of 1080-line HD as well.

Creating the Freeze Frame

Now let's make our freeze frame. The duration isn't that significant as we can always trim the clip after editing it, but it is generally a good idea to make these longer than we think we'll need so they're easier to edit into the sequence.

To create a freeze frame:

1. Choose CLIP > FREEZE FRAME > TWO FIELD FREEZE FRAMES > USING INTERPOLATED FIELD to set the render type for the freeze frame, as shown in Figure 4.2.

Figure 4.2
The freeze frame render options.

2. Choose **CLIP > FREEZE FRAME > 20 SECONDS**. As creating a freeze frame by default involves creating media, Media Composer displays a dialog box asking where to store the media. (See Figure 4.3.)

Figure 4.3
Render drive selection.

3. It is generally a good idea to store the rendered media on the same drive as the rest of your media. There are some exceptions to this rule, particularly when working with shared storage, but unless you are using this book in a classroom and your instructor tells you otherwise, select the drive that contains the course media and click **OK** to create the freeze frame.

Tip: To make it easier to create freeze frames, you may want to map the menu option to create a freeze frame of a specific length to the keyboard or the Source-side Composer window buttons.

4. Since you have more than one bin open, Media Composer next asks where to store the freeze frame clip. (See Figure 4.4.) Select the bin to save to and click **OK**.

Figure 4.4
Bin selection.

Look at the bin you selected. Freeze frame clips have a special clip icon so that they are easily distinguishable from regular clips. (See Figure 4.5.) To make it easy to work with, the freeze frame we just created has been automatically loaded into the Source monitor.

Figure 4.5
Freeze frame in bin.

Making the Edit

Finally, let's edit the freeze frame into our Timeline, replacing the clip we are currently parked on.

To edit the freeze frame into the sequence:

1. Click the Program monitor in the Composer window to make the sequence active.

2. Turn on **V1** if it isn't already active, and turn off all audio and other video tracks.

3. Click the **Mark Clip** button (see Figure 4.6) at the top of the Timeline or press **T** on the keyboard to mark the video clip.

Figure 4.6
Mark Clip button.

4. Move the play bar to the center of the freeze frame in the Source monitor. This step isn't absolutely necessary, but it does make it easier to trim the clip later on.

5. Click the **Overwrite Edit** button (see Figure 4.7) in the Composer window between the two monitors or press the **B** key on the keyboard to replace the shot.

Figure 4.7
Overwrite Edit button.

6. Take a look at the clip on the Timeline. Notice that FF has been appended to the name of the clip but that the freeze frame clip does not have any effect icon. Play through this portion of the sequence to see the freeze frame in context with the material around it.

Creating Motion Effects

With Motion effects, you control the frame rate at which a clip plays, resulting in fast, slow, or jerky motion. When creating Motion effects, the more noticeable the motion is in a clip, the more careful you should be when you choose a frame rate or render method. For example, if someone is running quickly through the frame, not all frame rates and render methods will create acceptable results.

As with freeze frames, Motion effects are generated from clips in the Source monitor, rather than clips already edited into a sequence.

This time, rather than choosing a source clip from a bin, let's generate a Motion effect from a clip already in the sequence.

To create a Motion effect with a clip already edited into the sequence:

1. Choose **TOOLS > MARKERS** to open the Markers window.

2. Double-click the marker named **MOTION EFFECT** to jump to that location in the Timeline.

3. Ensure that **V1** is active, and turn off all audio and other video tracks.

4. The frame we start the Motion effect with is located at the head of the edit. Click the **MATCH FRAME** button (see Figure 4.8) in the Composer window **FAST** menu.

Figure 4.8
Match Frame button.

5. The clip that was edited into the sequence is loaded into the Source monitor and the frame that you were parked on in the sequence is displayed and marked with an IN point. Now let's create a Motion effect from that clip. Click the **MOTION EFFECT** button (see Figure 4.9) in the Composer window **FAST** menu. The Motion Effect dialog box appears. (See Figure 4.10.)

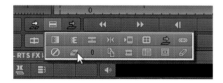

Figure 4.9
Motion Effect button.

Figure 4.10
Motion Effect dialog box.

Note: You cannot use the Motion Effect button in the Timeline palette to create a Motion effect. This button is used only to modify a Motion effect that has already been created in the sequence.

6. We'd like to add an element of drama by speeding up the setting of the sun. Set the SPEED PERCENTAGE to **1500%**.

The footage that we are working with was captured with progressive format, so we should use Both Fields.

Setting the Proper Render Method

As with the freeze frame, we need to set the proper render method. Because the final effect will be moving, however, this choice is even more important than it is for freeze frames. The following options are available:

- **Duplicated Field.** The default choice. This option reduces the vertical resolution by half because it drops one field of the image, resulting in a lower-quality image. This option does not require rendering (which is probably why it's the default). Be aware that Duplicated Field should never be used in a project intended for broadcast (unless it is deliberately used to create a stylization) as it cuts the video's vertical resolution in half. It is only intended for offline use.

- **Both Fields.** Good for shots without interfield motion, progressive video (where both fields are from the same film frame or time instance), and still shots. For best results, you should also use evenly divisible frame rates with this option.

- **Interpolated Field.** Calculates the Motion effect at the field level rather than the frame level by combining field line pairs. Because the system considers all fields when creating the effect, the smoothest motion results. This method is best for video-originated material or film-originated material shot at 24 fps. Because it combines fields to create new fields, the resulting Motion effect may be slightly soft.

- **VTR-Style.** Calculates the Motion effect at the field level rather than the frame level by shifting field information by a scan line. This creates very smooth Motion effects without any reduction in detail. At very slow speeds, a slight vertical jitter (due to the field shifts) may be noticeable.

To set the Motion effect render option and generate the effect:

1. Choose **BOTH FIELDS** as the render option for the Motion effect. With the exception of reverse Motion effects and very high-speed Motion effects, it is not typically necessary to render Motion effects if you are editing on modern computer hardware and drives. If we were slowing down the clip or speeding it up by a factor of three or five, we would not have to render the clip. But since we are increasing the speed by a factor of 15, we should render the clip.

Tip: Even though reverse and high-speed Motion effects cannot play in real time without being rendered, you can scrub through them prior to rendering.

2. Select **CREATE AND RENDER** to generate the Motion effect. As with the freeze frame, an additional dialog box will be displayed, allowing you to choose the bin to store the newly created Motion effect.

3. Select the bin you wish to save to and click **OK**. A progress bar is displayed while the clip is rendered. This should take only a few seconds.

4. Look at the bin you selected. Motion effect clips have the same clip icon as a freeze frame but are named to indicate the change in frame rate applied to the clip. (See Figure 4.11.) As with freeze frames, the newly created clip is automatically loaded into the Source monitor.

Figure 4.11
Motion effect in bin.

Making the Edit

Finally, let's edit the Motion effect into our Timeline. As we did with the freeze frame, we are going to replace a clip in the sequence. To help you quickly jump to the right location, we've set a marker.

To edit the Motion effect into the bin:

1. Click the Record monitor in the Composer window to make the sequence active.

2. Ensure that **V1** is active and turn off all audio and other video tracks.

3. Click the **Mark Clip** button at the top of the Timeline or press **T** on the keyboard to mark the video clip.

4. Click the **Overwrite Edit** button in the Composer window between the two monitors or press the **B** key on the keyboard to replace the shot.

5. Play through this area of the sequence to see the completed effect.

Take a look at the edit we just made on the Timeline. Like other effects, and unlike freeze frames, Motion effects have an icon. This icon not only tells us that the clip is a Motion effect, but it also tells us the render method used to generate it. This extra bit of information is extremely useful in the later stages of editing, especially if a previous editor used the wrong type of Motion effect—for example, Duplicated Field. The following shows the different icons and what they indicate.

Icon	Render Method
	Duplicated Field
	Both Fields
	Interpolated Field
	VTR-Style

Creating Motion Effects Using Fit to Fill

Motion effects can also be created using the Fit to Fill button. Fit to Fill will create a Motion effect of the source clip and then edit the resulting effect into the Timeline. The marked durations of the source clip and the sequence are used to determine the Motion effect rate. Be aware that creating Motion effects in this way can cause fractional frame rates that may not produce as good a result as even frame rates. Despite this, they can still be an efficient way to generate things like a very high-speed version of a long, slow shot. The Fit to Fill command creates Motion effects using the Both Fields rendering method.

Let's redo the effect we just created, this time using the Fit to Fill command to help us use the entire sunset action, rather than just a speeded-up version of a portion of it.

To create a Fit to Fill Motion effect:

1. Double-click on the **Motion Effect** marker to jump to that location in the Timeline.

2. Ensure that **V1** is active, and turn off all audio and other video tracks.

3. Click the **MARK CLIP** button at the top of the Timeline or press **T** on the keyboard to mark the video clip in the sequence.

4. As the locator was placed on the very first frame of the clip we want to replace, we can use the Match Frame button to bring the original clip up in the Source monitor. Click the **MATCH FRAME** button in the Composer window **FAST** menu.

5. When Match Frame is used on a Motion effect, the effect is brought up in the Source monitor as that is the "source" that was edited into the Timeline. We want, however, to use the source clip from which the Motion effect was generated. When an effect clip is loaded into the Source monitor, we can use Match Frame on that effect clip to bring up the source for the effect. Click the **MATCH FRAME** button again in the Composer window **FAST** menu.

Tip: Since the Source monitor was active within the Composer window, the Fast menu command operates on it (which contains the Motion effect clip) rather than the sequence.

6. We'd like to use the material in the clip from the frame we matched all the way to the end of the clip. Since the Match Frame button marks an IN at the frame we matched, we can simply jump to the end of the clip and mark an OUT. Press the **END** key on the keyboard to move to the end of the clip.

7. Press either the **R** or **O** key on the keyboard to mark an OUT. The Fit to Fill is not mapped by default to any key on the keyboard or onscreen button. It can, however, be accessed via the Command palette.

8. Choose **TOOLS > COMMAND PALETTE** to open the Command palette.

9. Click the **EDIT** button at the top of the palette to display the Edit pane. The Fit to Fill button is located at the bottom of the second column of commands. (See Figure 4.12.)

Figure 4.12
Fit to Fill button.

10. Before we can use the button we must make sure the Command palette is in Active Palette mode. The other two buttons are used to map commands to either the keyboard or the onscreen buttons. The Active Palette button should be illuminated to indicate that it is selected. If it is not (for example, because one of the other buttons is selected), you have to click it to select it. If necessary, click the **ACTIVE PALETTE** button at the bottom of the Command palette.

11. Click the **FIT TO FILL** button to perform the edit. A dialog box will be displayed to choose the bin to store the newly created Motion effect clip.

12. Select the desired bin and click **OK**. The Motion effect is rendered and edited into the sequence. Fit to Fill Motion effects are always rendered using the previously selected render method, and the medium is rendered to the default location on your system. Depending on your system configuration, this may be the internal hard drive or an external media drive.

13. Play through this area of the sequence to see the completed effect.

Timewarp Effects

Timewarp effects are an advanced type of Motion effect. They differ from traditional Motion effects in several ways:

■ Timewarp effects are applied to segments in a sequence, not to original source clips. When a regular Motion effect is created, its duration is determined by the motion rate selected. Timewarp effects do not change the duration of a segment in the Timeline. The duration is modified using standard trim techniques.

■ Timewarp effects do not have a fixed rate of speed. The speed can be varied over time. The editor can use keyframes to set multiple rates of speed, and the system will smoothly ramp between them. Optionally, the editor can specify start and end frames, and the system will calculate the rate required.

■ Timewarp effects contain additional, higher-quality render methods. These new methods add the capability to blend field data, resulting in much smoother motion.

Timewarp Preset Effects

Avid Media Composer ships with a number of prebuilt Timewarp effects. These are accessible via the Timewarp category in the Effect Palette. (See Figure 4.13.)

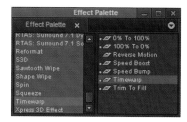

Figure 4.13
Effect Palette, Timewarp category.

Most of the preset effects are designed to generate variable-speed Motion effects. For example, the 0% to 100% preset ramps the speed gradually between a freeze frame and the clip's native speed. The 100% to 0% preset does the opposite, gradually slowing down from the clip's native speed until stopping at a freeze frame.

An extremely useful preset is Reverse Motion. This enables you to instantly reverse the motion of a clip that you've already inserted into the Timeline. Depending on the type of work you do, this may become one of your "go-to" effects.

Finally, among the preset effects you'll also find an effect called Timewarp, which does nothing by default. It provides access to the full capabilities of the Timewarp effect.

Applying a Reverse Motion Timewarp Preset

Though the use of a Reverse Motion effect may often seem obvious, sometimes it can be used as a subtle way to actually improve the perceived motion of a clip in the sequence.

To apply a Reverse Motion Timewarp preset:

1. Click the Markers window.

Tip: You can choose Tools > Markers to open this window if you can't readily locate it.

2. Double-click the marker named **REVERSE** to jump to that location in the Timeline.

3. Play through the clip and notice that, due to camera movement, the runners appear to be moving backward. Let's see if reversing the motion makes the shot work more effectively.

4. Choose **Tools > Effect Palette** to open the Effect Palette.

5. Click the **Timewarp** category.

6. Select the **Reverse Motion** preset and drag it to the **Runners, Focus on Runner 1** clip. Two key changes occur. First, the name of the clip has been appended with (–100%) to indicate that the clip has been reversed. Second, there is a blue dot in the lower-right corner of the effect icon. This blue dot indicates that the effect cannot be played in real time and must be rendered. Let's render the effect so we can see the result.

7. Make sure the position indicator is parked on the clip and click the **Render Effect** button in the Timeline button bar. (See Figure 4.14.) The Choose Render Drive dialog box will appear.

Figure 4.14
Render effect.

8. Choose the appropriate render drive and click **OK** to render the effect.

9. Play through this portion of the sequence to see the result.

Creating a Timewarp Freeze Frame

As we mentioned earlier, the Timewarp is a very powerful effect and includes the ability to keyframe Motion effects. Let's take advantage of this capability to create a version of the freeze frame that can be created entirely from within the sequence. This more modern version of the freeze frame has several advantages over the traditional freeze frame:

■ The rendering method can be changed without re-creating the effect.

■ It can be easily modified to change the frame that is frozen, which can help avoid problems that may be encountered in later stages of post-production.

■ It is much easier to run and therefore much easier for the online editor to troubleshoot and correct problems.

In this case, rather than doing a complete shot as a freeze frame as we did earlier, we're going to take advantage of the ease of creation and use this effect to correct an editorial problem.

To create a Timewarp freeze frame:

1. Click the Markers window.

2. Double-click the marker named Timewarp Freeze Frame to jump to that location in the Timeline.

3. Play through the clip. The camera operator turns at the end of the shot, creating an undesired pan. The motion is only a few frames long, but perhaps the shot would work better if we covered the unwanted pan with a freeze frame.

Tip: This type of corrective effect is quite common during the online or finishing stage of editing, especially if the audio is locked and the shot cannot be slipped or trimmed to correct the problem. If you watch television reality or documentary shows and look for these types of effects, you'll start to notice them in nearly every show. This is just one of the effect tricks in the online editor's bag to fix problems in the program.

4. Click the Markers window and double-click the Timewarp Freeze Frame marker again to jump to the frame where we wish to apply the Timewarp freeze frame.

5. Enable track V1 and make sure that all other tracks are disabled.

6. Choose Tools > Effect Palette to open the Effect Palette.

7. Click the Timewarp category.

8. Select the Timewarp effect and drag it to the Agadez, Runners, Reunion clip.

Modifying the Timewarp Effect

If you play through the newly added effect, you'll notice that nothing has apparently changed. By default, the Timewarp effect does essentially nothing, just like other effects such as Resize. We must manipulate its parameters to create the effect. But unlike other effects, the Timewarp effect does not use the Effect Editor; instead, it has its own editor. This is due to the unique characteristics of a Timewarp effect.

To prepare to edit the Timewarp effect:

1. Click the Markers window.

2. Double-click the marker named Timewarp Freeze Frame to jump to that location in the Timeline.

3. Click either the **EFFECT MODE** or **MOTION EFFECT EDITOR** button in the Timeline palette. (See Figure 4.15.) The Motion Effect Editor opens. (See Figure 4.16.)

Figure 4.15
Timeline palette.

Figure 4.16
Motion Effect Editor.

Although some of the function in this window will be immediately apparent from your experience with the traditional Motion Effect dialog box, the Motion Effect Editor manipulates the effect via two pop-out graphs: the speed graph and the position graph. (See Figure 4.17.) We'll work with only the speed graph in this course.

Figure 4.17
Speed Graph and Position Graph buttons.

4. Click the **SPEED GRAPH** button to expand the Motion Effect Editor window to reveal the speed graph, as shown in Figure 4.18.

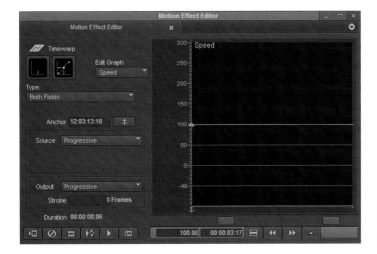

Figure 4.18
Motion Effect Editor with the
speed graph displayed.

Understanding the Speed Graph

The speed graph allows you to set the speed of the Timewarp effect using keyframes. For illustrative purposes, Figure 4.19 uses the graph of the 100% to 0% Timewarp preset.

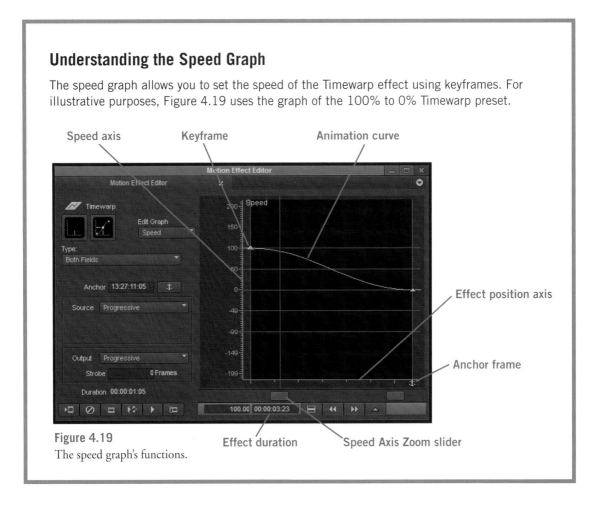

Figure 4.19
The speed graph's functions.

- **Speed axis.** Displays a range of speeds available. 100 is equal to sound speed (29.97 fps in NTSC, 25 fps in PAL). By default, the speed axis displays speeds between 300% and –100%.

- **Speed Axis Zoom slider.** Zooms in and out on the speed axis. Drag left to reveal additional rates of speed and right to show fewer rates of speed.

- **Effect position axis.** Displays position information. By default, the effect position axis displays only the duration of the effect.

- **Position Axis Zoom slider.** Zooms in and out on the effect position axis. Drag left to reveal position information beyond the effect duration and right to zoom in on the effect duration.

- **Effect duration.** The duration of the effect is displayed as black in the position graph. Areas outside of the effect duration are displayed as dark gray. Dark purple vertical lines indicate the beginning and end of the effect duration.

- **Animation curve.** Indicates the speed or change in speed created with the Timewarp effect. Drag the position indicator to see the speed at any point along the curve.

- **Keyframe.** Used to set the rate of speed at a given position.

- **Anchor frame.** Indicates the point where the source footage is anchored in the effect.

Note that after zooming in and out, the curve can often be offset and partially offscreen. To reposition the curve in the image, hold down the Alt key (Windows) or Option key (Mac) and drag the graph to the desired position.

Creating the Freeze Frame

Now let's create the freeze frame. As you can see, there is a single keyframe on the speed graph, at the beginning of the effect. All Timewarp effects have this single keyframe. Additional keyframes can be added, just as they can in other effects, and we want to add a new keyframe at the marker's position.

To turn this effect into a keyframe, we simply need to change the value of this keyframe from 100 to 0 and can do so by dragging the keyframe downward to the zero value on the speed, or Y, axis.

To create the freeze frame:

1. Make sure you are parked on the frame with the marker.

2. Click the **Add Keyframe** button in the lower-right region of the Motion Effect Editor to add a keyframe to the current frame. (See Figure 4.20.)

Figure 4.20
Add Keyframe button.

3. Before we go any further, we want to ensure that the source frame we are parked on is always the frame that the freeze frame occurs on. We can do this by setting this keyframe as the anchor frame. This will "anchor" this frame in the source to this point in the Timeline. Click the SET ANCHOR button on the left side of the Motion Effect Editor to set the selected keyframe to the anchor. (See Figure 4.21.)

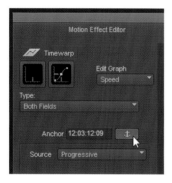

Figure 4.21
Set Anchor button.

Tip: Any time you want to ensure that a Timewarp does not shift the position of a specific frame, you should set a keyframe at that frame and then set an anchor. This is especially useful when you want to sync a particular action in the effect to a cue in the music. Note that you can only have one anchor in a Timewarp effect.

4. Now let's change the keyframe's speed to zero (0) so that the picture freezes at this frame. Click the pink keyframe and drag it downward until you reach the zero value. The keyframe snaps to the zero value. You can also see the exact value you are dragging to via the green indicator at the top of the graph. This indicator replaces the word "Speed" while you are dragging a keyframe as shown in Figure 4.22.

Play through the effect. That isn't exactly what we wanted, is it? Rather than instantly freezing at the frame with the marker, the clip gradually slows down until it freezes at the frame. What we want instead is for the clip to play at full speed *until* it reaches the marker and then instantly freeze.

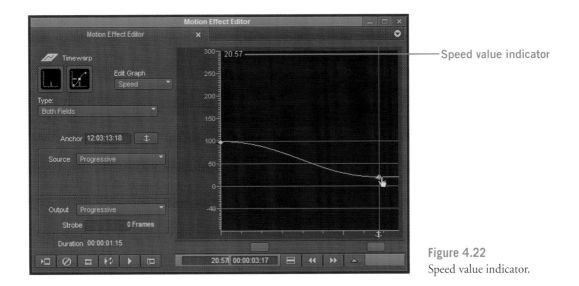

Figure 4.22
Speed value indicator.

The reason it slows down gradually between the two keyframes is that, by default, a smooth change in speed occurs between any two keyframes. Although this is the default type of keyframe, there are actually four different types of keyframes:

■ **Linear.** Creates a direct path between two keyframe values. In a linear keyframe, the rate of change is continuous between the two keyframes, and there is no gradual acceleration (ease-in) or deceleration (ease-out) from one keyframe into another. (See Figure 4.23.)

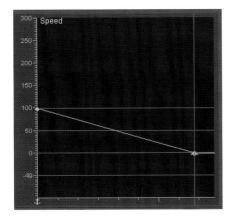

Figure 4.23
Linear keyframes.

■ **Spline.** Creates a path with a natural ease-in and ease-out at every keyframe. The amount of ease-in and ease-out is automatically calculated to create a smooth transition into and out of keyframes and cannot be adjusted. (See Figure 4.24.)

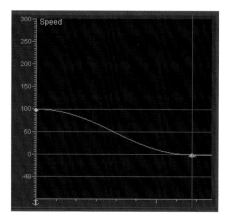

Figure 4.24
Spline keyframes.

■ **Bézier.** Creates a path with a natural ease-in and ease-out at every keyframe. Unlike spline interpolation, the shape of the animation curve can be adjusted on either side of the keyframe by manipulating the Bézier curve handles. (See Figure 4.25.) Bézier curves are beyond the scope of this book, but you can learn more about them in the *Avid Media Composer Effects Guide*.

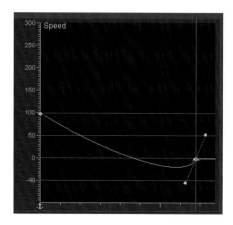

Figure 4.25
Bézier keyframes.

■ **Shelf.** Holds a keyframe's value until the next keyframe. This interpolation type is used to cause the parameter to jump instantly from one value to another. (See Figure 4.26.)

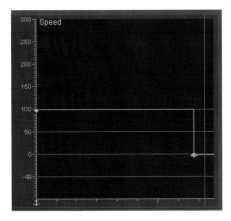

Figure 4.26
Shelf keyframes.

This last type of keyframe is what we want for our effect. It will keep the clip playing at full speed until our keyframe, at which point the clip will instantly freeze.

To configure the effect to instantly freeze:

1. Right-click the second keyframe in the speed graph and select **SHELF** from the pop-up menu, as shown in Figure 4.27. The graph changes to reflect the new keyframe type.

Figure 4.27
Keyframe pop-up menu.

2. Confirm that the render type is set to **BOTH FIELDS**. Since the source footage for this project is 23.976p, you should use this option.

3. Play through this area of the sequence to see the effect you applied. The freeze frame may be very obvious to you, but that is because you are aware that it is there. If you play through it several times, you brain will adjust, and it will no longer be as apparent.

Tip: Now that you've created this effect, if you wish to change the frame at
      which the freeze occurs, you can simply move the keyframe to another point.
      Hold the Alt+Shift (Windows) or Option+Shift (Mac) keys down while dragging
      the keyframe to move it to an earlier or later frame in the clip.

Corrective effects should be used sparingly until you become very familiar with
them. Certainly they can be extremely useful in the final stages of an edit, but they
should not become a crutch to cover problems that may be better solved editori-
ally, especially in the early stages of the edit.

Review/Discussion Questions

1. What are the three types of Motion effects?

2. How are freeze frames created?
    a. They are generated from a source clip.
    b. They are applied to a clip in the sequence.

3. Why is it important to set the freeze frame render type?

4. How are Motion effects created?
    a. They are generated from a source clip.
    b. They are applied to a clip in the sequence.

5. How does creating a Motion effect via the Fit to Fill command differ
    from creating one via the Motion Effect command?

6. How are Timewarp effects created?
    a. They are generated from a source clip.
    b. They are applied to a clip in the sequence.

7. What are the benefits of creating a Timewarp freeze frame versus a
    traditional freeze frame?

8. What are the four different types of keyframes?

9. Which keyframe is the most appropriate to use for a Timewarp freeze
    frame?

Motion Effects

Now it is time for you to apply what you've learned and use Timewarp effects to add some drama to the opening of an act from an episode of *Hell's Kitchen*. Your job is to add Timewarps to the second, third, and fourth shots in the sequence so that they begin at a very fast rate of speed but are playing at full (100%) speed when they hit the frames with the markers.

Media Used:

Hell's Kitchen

Duration:

20 minutes

GOALS

- Create a series of Timewarp effects whose motion is synchronized with anchor frames to specific locations in the Timeline

- Use different keyframe types to create different types of motion in the effect

For this exercise, you'll use the Hells Kitchen PT2 project, found in the HK Exercises bin. Open the HK Exercises sequence. Here are the producer's notes for each of the shots:

■ **Second shot.** The shot should begin with the 'copter shot far above the entrance and quickly fly in to the marked location. At that point, it should continue playing, but at 100% speed. The transition should be smooth but dramatic.

■ **Third shot.** The shot should begin zoomed in tight on the fire tree and out of focus. Then it should pull in quickly but return to 100% speed at the marked frame. The transition should be smooth, just as if someone simultaneously quickly zoomed in and pulled focus.

■ **Fourth shot.** The shot should begin with a rapid pan around the restaurant. This pan should stop abruptly at the marked frame. We want it to look somewhat mechanical, rather than smooth.

To accomplish these effects you will need to use the following skills you learned during this lesson:

■ Use Match Frame to bring up the source for a sequence edit in the Source monitor. This will help you see what material you have to work with.

■ Create anchor frames to lock specific frames in position.

■ Change keyframe types to create different transitions at keyframes.

Color Treating and Correcting

In this lesson we will look at ways that we can take what was originally shot and modify it either to create a specific look or to make it more accurately reflect what the subject looked like. We will look at the Color Effect, an effect with a unique set of parameters that lets us modify the look of an image, and the automatic correction tools within the Color Correction mode.

Media Used: Running the Sahara

Duration: 45 minutes

GOALS

- Use the Color Effect to create a variety of color treatments
- Identify the risks associated with the Color Effect
- Learn when to use the Safe Color Limiter
- Learn how to use the automatic color correction tools

Modifying the Look of a Shot

It is extremely rare that a program goes from camera to edit to screen without some or all of the shots being corrected or treated. There are a number of reasons for this, including:

- A scene was shot with multiple cameras of different makes, and each captured the images a bit differently.

- A scene was shot with one or more cameras not properly white balanced.

- The camera's auto-correction circuits inadvertently "fixed" a scene improperly, and what was recorded does not match what the subject really looks like.

- The cameraman deliberately captured the scene with low contrast so he could capture the maximum grayscale, expecting that the shot would be "fixed in post."

- The director or editor wants a shot to have a specific look that could not be captured in the camera.

Avid Media Composer has tools at your disposal to make these types of adjustments and corrections. The two primary tools are the Color Effect and Color Correction mode. In addition, there are a number of AVX plug-in effects that can be added to your system that are essential tools in an editor's arsenal, including GenArts Sapphire and Boris Continuum Complete. We will discuss using AVX plug-ins in Appendix A, "Using AVX Third-Party Plug-ins."

Let's look at the two built-in tools, starting with the Color Effect.

Creating Color Treatments

Though the Color Effect can be used for corrective work, we typically use Color Correction mode for that type of work. Instead, the Color Effect is generally used just for color treatments. Let's look at how it can be used to create a few different types of treatments.

To use the Color Effect to create treatments:

1. If the Running the Sahara project is not open from the last lesson, open Media Composer, select the **Running the Sahara** project on the left side of the Open Project dialog box, and click the **Open** button.

   The Project window opens and lists all the bins associated with this project. The bin you'll use in this lesson is the RTS PT2 FX Sequences bin, which contains a number of sequences you'll use throughout this book.

2. Double-click the **RTS PT2 FX Sᴇǫᴜᴇɴᴄᴇs** bin in the Project window to open it.

We'd like to create a freeze frame of a clip already edited into the sequence. Fortunately, that's very easy to do.

3. In the RTS PT2 FX Sequences bin window, double-click the **RTS FX PT2 Lᴇssᴏɴ 05** sequence. The sequence appears in the Record monitor.

Creating a Black and White Image

You might think that creating a black and white image is as easy as removing all of the color. But it actually involves a bit more than that. That's because a good black and white image needs a proper balance of the grayscale, and often that isn't what you're left with when you remove all of the color.

To create a black and white image:

1. Park on the first clip in the **RTS FX PT2 Lᴇssᴏɴ 05** sequence. Let's make this shot black and white.

2. Choose **Tᴏᴏʟs > Eғғᴇᴄᴛ Pᴀʟᴇᴛᴛᴇ** to open the Effect Palette.

3. On the left side of the palette, click the **Iᴍᴀɢᴇ** category.

4. Click and drag the **Cᴏʟᴏʀ Eғғᴇᴄᴛ** from the right side of the palette (see Figure 5.1) to the first clip in the Timeline.

Figure 5.1
The Color Effect in the Image category.

5. Enter Effect mode. The Effect Editor opens, displaying the available effect parameters within the Color Effect, as shown in Figure 5.2.

6. Locate the **Cʜʀᴏᴍᴀ Aᴅᴊᴜsᴛ** parameter group and drag the **Sᴀᴛ** (Saturation) slider all the way to the left to remove all of the color from the clip.

7. Play through the clip.

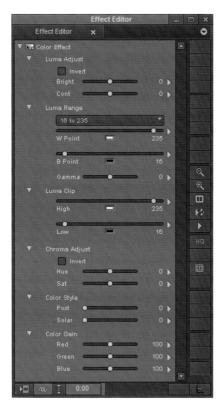

Figure 5.2
The Color Effect's parameters.

One of the problems with this clip is that it is quite dark. As a result, the black and white image is composed of lower- to mid-grayscale values and appears quite muddy. To create a good black and white image, we need the tones to be more widely distributed from black to white.

While it might seem that the tool to use for this is Contrast, the problem with Contrast is that it moves the blacks and whites by equal amounts either in or out from the midtones. Usually that isn't what a shot requires. Instead, we want to manipulate lighter grays and darker grays independently so that they can be adjusted the amount that each requires. To do this, we can use the Luma Range parameter group. (See Figure 5.3.)

Figure 5.3
The Luma Range parameter group.

There are three parameters within Luma Range: B Point (for black point), W Point (for white point), and Gamma. B Point and W Point define the whitest white and the blackest black in the image. By default they are set to the values of 16 for black and 235 for white. These values correspond to the digital bit values for video black and video white and are defined in video standards as the displayed limits for the grayscale. They are used not only by broadcasters but also by television manufacturers to calibrate the minimum and maximum values that will be displayed. Although it is possible to define blacks below 16 and whites above 235, these values are usually not visible. Indeed, broadcasters are especially picky about black levels and may reject a program that has values below video black.

Tip: The pop-up menu at the top of the Luma Range parameter group sets the display limits for all of the parameters in this group. As long as the default of 16–235 is selected in this menu, it is not possible to exceed these values using Luma Range. Instead, values that occur beyond these limits are "crushed" at those limits.

Gamma adjusts the tones between the white and black points. It is sometimes mistakenly referred to as the midtone adjustment, but it actually adjusts all colors from the black point to the white point using what is referred to as a *response curve.*

An increase in gamma will brighten the midrange tones the most but will also brighten all other tones. The effect then will gradually fall off the further the tones are from the middle. Figure 5.4 shows what basic gamma curves look like and how they affect the dark, midtone, and light areas of an image.

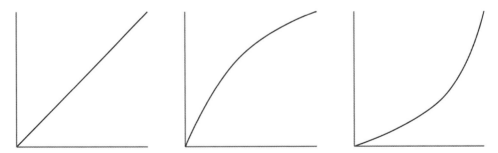

Figure 5.4
Normal gamma, increased gamma, and reduced gamma curves.

Finishing the Black and White Look

Now let's finish our black and white look using the Luma Range parameters. The image needs a good white and black, so let's use the B Point and W Point settings to establish a nice tonal range.

To finish the black and white look:

1. Set **W Point** setting to **175** and **B Point** setting to **35**.

   Notice how much better our image looks already. With a well-defined black and white we have a much more pleasing image. But the image is still weighted too much toward the lower middle grays. We can correct that by raising the gamma.

2. Set **Gamma** to **25**.

3. Play through the clip.

It looks a lot better now, doesn't it? Previously, the man was quite indistinct from the background. Now he stands out nicely. Great job!

The numbers provided work for this shot, but you'll have to experiment with other shots to determine what values work best for a given image.

Learning how to get a good black and white look is one of the core fundamentals in color correction and is the key to making a shot look good. To see what we mean, let's go one step further and restore the color to the image. To make this easy to see, the same shot has been edited twice into the lesson sequence.

To restore the color:

1. Set the **Sat** (saturation) parameter back to **0** (zero) to restore the color.

2. Exit Effect mode and play through this clip and the repeat that follows. Notice how much better the first image looks than the image you started with. However, since the image is now brighter, the color doesn't appear as saturated as it was. Let's fix that by boosting the saturation.

3. Set the **Sat** parameter to **50**.

4. Exit Effect mode and play through the two clips.

Tip: This technique can be a great way to fix a shot that is muddy and indistinct. Until you become comfortable "seeing through the color" to the grayscale, you may want to use the technique of removing the color, getting the grayscale right, and then restoring the color.

Creating a Sepia Tone Treatment

Now let's move to the third clip in the sequence. Let's tint this clip with a sepia tone, to simulate the look of an old photograph.

To create a sepia tone treatment:

1. Park on the third clip in the sequence.

2. Add a **COLOR EFFECT** to it and enter Effect mode.

   Much as with the previous treatment, to create a sepia tone, we first need to get a good-looking black and white image. This time, though, we want to adjust the luminance values so that the image has the tonal range of an old, faded photograph. We can do this by pushing the image toward the lighter tonal range.

3. Set the **SAT** parameter to **0**.

   Unlike the previous clip, this one has good blacks and whites. We can skip setting the black and white points and move on to the gamma.

4. Set **GAMMA** to **40**.

   Now we have a nice "high tone" black and white image ready to be tinted. The Color Gain parameter group allows us to manipulate the image directly using the colors red, green, and blue. But how do those parameters affect the image?

Colors and Complements

Red, green, and blue are the *primary* colors of the video color space. These color spaces are generally referred to as either Rec.709 for high definition video or Rec.601 for standard definition video. Increasing a primary color adds it to the image. For example, increasing green makes the image greener.

What if we have a black and white image? How can you remove green where no green apparently exists? In actuality, reducing a primary color *adds* that color's *complement*. A complementary color is opposite in hue from the primary color. If you were to think of color as a wheel, a color's complement is 180° away from that color. In the video color space, the complement for red is cyan, the complement for green is magenta, and the complement for blue is yellow, as shown in Figure 5.5. Therefore, you can think of removing red as adding cyan, removing green as adding magenta, and removing blue as adding yellow.

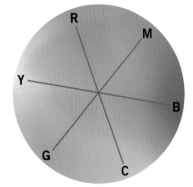

Figure 5.5
Video color space represented as a circle.

Adding the Sepia Tone

Sepia is a mix of red and yellow. Therefore, what we want to do is add red and remove blue (removing blue adds its complement, yellow). As mentioned earlier, we will use the Color Gain parameter group to add the tint.

To create a sepia tone:

1. Set the RED parameter to **120**.

2. Set the BLUE parameter to **85**.

   The amount of red and yellow you add will change the tint of sepia you create. Usually you want to add more red than yellow so that the sepia tone stays in the warm region. But the exact mix is really a matter of personal choice.

3. If desired, experiment with the RED and BLUE parameters to see what tint other combinations of the two create.

Creating a "Night Vision" Treatment

Take a look at the fourth shot in the Timeline. It was shot using very little light and, as a result, is quite indistinct. Since there's not a lot of information to work with, the producer thought it might look good if we made it look like it was originally shot with infrared "night vision" photography. Since the data we need wasn't recorded, we cannot easily simulate the actual tone response of an infrared camera. However, we can create a look that simulates infrared photography and perhaps improve the shot while we're at it.

Just as with the other treatments, we need to first get a good grayscale image. The problem with this shot is that, except for around the campfire, there really aren't a lot of tones other than slight variations of dark gray. That's okay, as the look is mostly dark tones except for very bright, hot sources (such as the fire), but we still need to open up the tones a bit to make it easier to see the interview subject.

To create a "night vision" treatment:

1. Park on the fourth clip in the Timeline (RUNNER 1 NIGHT INT) and apply a COLOR EFFECT to it.

2. As with the other treatments, set SAT to **0** (zero). Now let's try to bring some detail out of the image.

3. Set GAMMA to **30**. While that brightens up the image, there aren't any dark blacks in the image now. We need to correct that by changing the black point.

4. Set the **B Point** setting to **42**.

   That looks better. We've stretched the blacks out a bit, and the interview subject is a bit more distinct, but the shot could still have better contrast. Let's see what happens when we tint the shot.

5. Set the **Green** color gain to **150**.

   See how adding green gives us more apparent contrast? That's because increasing the green channel actually increases the value of the data within the green channel. Due to the nature of digital video, adjusting the green channel has the most direct impact on the image contrast and brightness. But the green isn't the intense color that is often associated with night vision photography. We can improve the green by removing the other two primary colors.

6. Set the **Red** and **Blue** color gains to **75**. That looks much better.

7. Play through the clip to see the finished effect.

Color Effect and Video Output

When you use the Color Effect, you run the risk of creating effects that exceed the signal limits allowed for a broadcast program. If you are just producing something for the Web, this isn't a big deal, but if you are delivering a program that will be broadcast by an on-air or cable/satellite network, you need to pay attention to the signal that is generated by the Color Effect.

The top two parameter groups—Luma Adjust and Luma Range—aren't very risky because after them comes the Luma Clip parameter group. This will clip the levels at video black and video white. (Remember that the values 16 and 235 are equivalent to video black and video white.) But the Chroma Adjust, Chroma Style, and Color Gain parameter groups all come after the Luma Clip group. If you make adjustments here, you might create "illegal" color levels.

Fortunately, Media Composer includes a Safe Color Limiter effect that can be stacked on top of a Color Effect to prevent the output of the effect from exceeding the standard limits applied by virtually all broadcasters. This effect is located in the Image category in the Effect Palette. (See Figure 5.6.) The Safe Color Limiter is typically applied by placing it over the shots that require limiting, usually on a higher track. We will return to this effect and show how to place and configure it in Lesson 7, "Multilayer Effects."

Figure 5.6
The Safe Color Limiter effect.

Introduction to Color Correction

Avid Media Composer's Color Correction mode is the "big brother" to the Color Effect. Nearly all of the adjustments available in the Color Effect are also available in Color Correction mode, if perhaps presented in a different way. Color Correction mode also uses a special set of controls that provide powerful ways to manipulate the colors and tones of the shots in a sequence.

Color Correction Mode

You access Color Correction mode using one of the following:

■ Click the Color Correction Mode button in the Timeline palette, as shown in Figure 5.7.

■ Choose Windows > Workspaces > Color Correction.

Figure 5.7
Color Correction Mode button.

Tip: You can also map the Color Correction Mode button to a key from the CC tab in the Command palette. If you are using the Training User settings, Color Correction mode has been mapped to the F12 key.

When you enter Color Correction mode, the Composer monitor shifts to a three-monitor view, and a new Color Correction tool is positioned between the Composer and Timeline windows, as shown in Figure 5.8.

The three monitors in the Composer window are configured by default to show the shot you are working with in the center monitor, the shot preceding it in the Timeline to the left, and the shot following it to the right.

The Color Correction tool has two adjustment groups, which are available via the HSL (see Figure 5.9) and Curves (see Figure 5.10) tabs.

The HSL group contains adjustments that independently manipulate the hue, saturation, and luminance of the image. This allows you to adjust the color (hue and saturation) without affecting the grayscale (luminance), for example.

Figure 5.8
Color Correction mode.

Figure 5.9
HSL group.

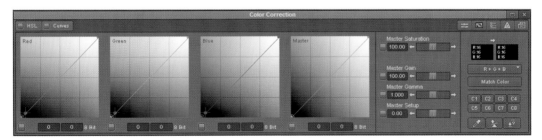

Figure 5.10
Curves group.

The Curves group contains adjustments that manipulate the red, green, and blue channels of the image. Unlike the HSL group adjustments, in Curves you are always simultaneously adjusting both color and grayscale. Let's take a brief look at its power by discussing the automatic color correction tools.

**In the Avid
Learning Series**

To learn how to use the powerful color grading tools available in Avid editing systems for professional color grading and finishing, check out the book in this series *Color Grading on Media Composer and Symphony 6*.

About Automatic Color Correction

Automatic corrections are easy to learn and apply and can remove common color problems in many images. When you use one of the automatic color corrections, the system analyzes the colors and tones of an image and makes adjustments to some of the color correction controls to attempt to "correct" for common color problems—similar to how most digital cameras automatically try to white-balance a scene.

Both color correction groups include buttons that allow you to make automatic color corrections to correct contrast problems, balance color, or remove color. Automatic color correction can help you learn how to recognize color problems in images and identify the types of adjustments that can be made to solve them.

Automatically Adjusting Contrast and Balance

Contrast problems are the most common problems you'll encounter. As we saw previously, creating a proper grayscale can be the most important adjustment you can make as it brings out detail that might otherwise be obscured. Just as common are white-balance problems, where the cameraman either didn't white balance the camera properly or was not able to do so while following the subject through different lighting. (For example, a shot may start inside with fluorescent lighting and then move outside with daylight lighting. If the cameraman had white balanced for the interior lighting, when he followed the subject outside, the camera would be improperly balanced for the exterior shots.)

When to Use Automatic Color Correction

Automatic color corrections may be useful while doing the offline edit, particularly if you need only to correct a basic color problem such as a color cast or if you need a quick and easy solution to an image problem.

Automatic color correction works best with shots that are close to correct. A good guideline is that the more severe the problem, the less likely it is that automatic color correction will produce the expected results.

When Not to Use Automatic Color Correction

Automatic color corrections are not recommended for online finishing work. If you are finishing, you should always use manual correction techniques for greatest accuracy and control. Manual corrections require more skill and practice but allow you more precise control over the final look of your images and give you a greater range of creative possibilities.

The major drawback of automatic color correction is that the system cannot see what's in the scene. It doesn't see landscape or faces; it can't differentiate between foreground and background; it only knows that there is some white, yellow, blue, and so on. It will make assumptions about the colors in the frame, assumptions that may or may not be correct.

There are many color correction problems that are not appropriate for automatic correction. Automatic color corrections might not provide useful results with the following:

- **Extreme light conditions.** If a significant area of an image is deliberately overexposed or underexposed, automatic color corrections may misunderstand the intent and produce an undesired result.

- **Extreme color balance problems.** Automatic color corrections might not provide the expected result on images that show extreme white-balance issues or in mixed-lighting conditions where part of the image is white balanced while other parts of the image are not.

- **Poorly calibrated video.** Automatic color corrections operate on images that are within normal limits for legal video levels and might not produce the expected results for video with areas of the image beyond video white or video black levels.

- **Images lacking the appropriate distinct white or black regions.** Automatic color corrections are only effective with images that have the appropriate content for calculating either white, black, or both, such as areas of strong highlight (white or close to white) and areas of strong shadow (black or close to black).

Automatic contrast and balance adjustments are available in both the Hue and Curves groups, as shown in Figures 5.11 and 5.12.

Figure 5.11
The contrast and balance adjustments in the HSL group are the buttons along the bottom.

Figure 5.12
The contrast and balance adjustments in the Curves group are the buttons along the bottom.

Let's take a look at the results that can be achieved with both sets of contrast and balance controls by correcting a couple of shots using both sets of tools and then comparing the results. First let's use the HSL group's controls.

To use auto correction in the HSL group:

1. Move the position indicator so that it is parked in the middle of the first of two clips named INJURY IN TENT.

    Because automatic color correction analyzes only the frame you are currently parked on, it is generally a good idea to correct when parked on a frame somewhere in the middle of the clip rather than the first or last frame, especially if there is a camera motion at the beginning or end of the clip.

2. Ensure that **V2** in the Timeline is inactive and that **V1** is active.

    Automatic color corrections are always applied to the highest active track and must be applied to a clip, not to filler. If the empty V2 track were active, the correction would have no effect.

3. Select the **HSL** tab and, if necessary, click the HUE OFFSETS subtab.

Tip: The HSL group contains two sets of adjustments, Controls and Hue Offsets. These two sets are accessed via the subtabs located below the two main group tabs. (See Figure 5.13.)

Figure 5.13
Controls and Hue Offsets subtabs.

4. Click the **Auto Contrast** button, shown in Figure 5.14.

Figure 5.14
Auto Contrast automatic correction button.

Auto Contrast automatic correction adjusts the black and white levels (known as *setup* and *gain*) to maximize the tonal range in the image. The darkest area in the current frame is set to video black, and the dominant bright area in the current frame is set to video white.

Note: **If the HSL group's Auto Contrast detects what it considers to be *specular highlights*—for example the light glint of the surface of water or an isolated area that is much brighter than the rest of the image—it will push those whites beyond video white. This isn't an issue most of the time, but may need to be compensated for with manual adjustments or the use of the Safe Color Limiter effect if going to broadcast.**

5. Click the **Auto Balance** button, shown in Figure 5.15.

Figure 5.15
Auto Balance automatic correction button.

Auto Balance automatic correction independently adjusts the white balance of the image's shadows, midtones, and highlights. These adjustments can be seen in the three ChromaWheel controls, shown in Figure 5.16. Notice that the crosshairs are no longer centered in the middle of the wheels, as compared to previous illustrations, but are now all slightly adjusted down and to the right.

Figure 5.16
ChromaWheel controls after Auto Balance is applied.

6. Play through the corrected clip and then the second **INJURY IN TENT** clip immediately afterward to compare the corrected and uncorrected shots.

   In this instance, the auto correction made a dramatic improvement in the shot.

7. So that we have another auto correction to compare to, let's move the position indicator so that it is parked in the middle of the first of two clips named **CAMEL RIDE**.

8. Click the **AUTO CONTRAST** button to correct the tonal range.

9. Click the **AUTO BALANCE** button to correct the white balance.

10. Play through the corrected clip and then the second **CAMEL RIDE** clip immediately afterward to compare the corrected and uncorrected shots.

    This time the correction is a bit more subtle, as the uncorrected shot was not as underexposed as the previous shot. As before, the auto corrections do a good job and certainly are an improvement over the uncorrected shot.

Now let's use the Auto Contrast and Auto Balance correction tools in the Curves group and see how the result compares to the auto corrections in the HSL group.

To use auto correction in the Curves group:

1. Move the position indicator so that it is parked in the middle of the second of two clips named **INJURY IN TENT**.

2. Select the **CURVES** tab.

3. Click the **AUTO BALANCE** button, shown in Figure 5.17.

Figure 5.17
Auto Balance automatic correction button.

Note: The Curves group contains four curves—red, green, blue, and master—
which are processed in order from left to right. Because of that order of
processing, to achieve the best results from auto corrections within the
Curves group, you should apply Auto Balance (which adjusts the red, green,
and blue curves) before Auto Contrast (which adjusts the master curve).
Note that this is opposite from the recommended order of application in
the HSL group.

In the Curves group, Auto Balance tries to balance the red, green, and blue channels. This is a very different approach from that used for the HSL group. Both are completely valid approaches, but depending on the conditions in a given clip, you may prefer the results of one or the other.

4. Click the **Auto Contrast** button, shown in Figure 5.18.

Figure 5.18
Auto Contrast automatic correction button.

5. Now move the position indicator so that it is parked in the middle of the second of two clips named **Camel ride**.

6. Click the **Auto Balance** button to correct the white balance of the shot.

7. Click the **Auto Contrast** button to correct the tonal range.

8. Now scrub through all four clips and compare the corrections made by the HSL group and the Curves group.

Depending on the calibration (or lack thereof) of the display you are looking at, you may notice that the HSL auto corrections appear to be warmer, and the Curves corrections appear to be cooler. It could be argued that the HSL group's auto corrections did a better job, but that's not always the case. It really depends on the nature of the shots to be corrected and the material that is visible in the frame. When in doubt, try them both!

User-Assisted White Balance Corrections

The Color Correction mode also has white balance correction tools known as the Remove Color Cast tools. These allow you to help the correction along by identifying areas of the image that should be neutral in tone. They can be used to enhance the results gained from the Auto Balance correction.

Using the Remove Color Cast Tools in the HSL Group

The HSL group has separate Remove Color Cast tools for the shadows, midtones, and highlights. These are the buttons marked with an eyedropper shown along the bottom of Figure 5.19.

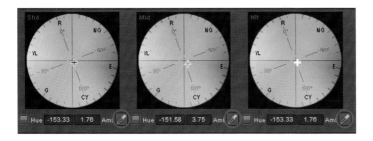

Figure 5.19
The HSL group Remove Color Cast tools are the buttons along the bottom that feature an eyedropper icon.

Each Remove Color Cast tool is associated with the ChromaWheel above it, and only the parts of the image that fall within the luminance range associated with each wheel are affected. Since the adjustments made with the Remove Color Cast tools are identical to those made by the Auto Balance tool, you can use them either in lieu of Auto Balance or to correct for an error made by Auto Balance.

It is certainly worth experimenting with these tools, but you'll find that in most images there might not be easily identifiable neutral tones for the three tonal ranges. Getting comfortable with these tools will take experimentation and practice.

Using the Remove Color Cast Tools in the Curves Group

There is a single Remove Color Cast tool in the Curves group, as shown in Figure 5.20.

Figure 5.20
The Curves group Remove Color Cast tool is the button along the bottom that features an eyedropper icon.

As compared to the HSL group, the Remove Color Cast tool in Curves performs a different function from the Auto Balance tool and can be quite useful to improve the results. For example, we noted earlier than the results from the two Curves group auto corrections seemed to be cool, compared to the HSL group corrections.

Whereas the Auto Balance balances the red, green, and blue channels by setting their low and high limits, Remove Color Cast changes the white balance by adding a control point between the low and high adjustments. This extra point can be very effective in removing an unwanted cast that can remain after the Auto Balance tool is used. Let's use the Remove Color Cast tool to correct for the blue/magenta cast left in the Camel ride clip after we used the Curves auto corrections.

To use the Remove Color Cast tool:

1. Move the position indicator to the beginning of the second of the two clips named **CAMEL RIDE** so that the gentleman wearing the white turban is clearly visible in the frame.

2. Click on the **REMOVE COLOR CAST** tool to select it.

3. Move the cursor (now shaped like an eyedropper) to a midtone region of the white scarf, as shown in Figure 5.21.

Figure 5.21
Remove Color Cast tool applied to the white scarf in the frame.

4. Click the mouse to instruct the tool to adjust the white balance based on the selected region.

    The shot warms up significantly, and the blue/magenta cast is removed. An additional control point is added to the red, green, and blue curves as shown in Figure 5.22.

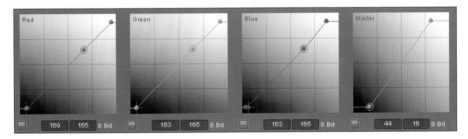

Figure 5.22
Curves group Remove Color Cast tool.

5. Scrub through the two **CAMEL RIDE** clips and compare the HSL and Curves group corrections.

    The two are now extremely similar. Depending on where you clicked on the white scarf, you may find that the HSL group correction is now slightly cooler than the Curves group correction.

6. (Optional) Press **CTRL+Z** (Windows) or **COMMAND+Z** (Mac) to undo the Remove Color Cast correction and experiment with the Remove Color Cast tool by clicking on other areas of the white scarf.

Tip: Always undo the Remove Color Cast result before performing it again. If you don't, you will gain an additional correction for each use of the tool, and the correction will not necessarily improve. Indeed, it is possible to generate some very unsatisfactory results!

Review/Discussion Questions

1. What are some of the reasons that you may need to correct or treat one or more shots in a sequence?

2. Why is it important to get a good tonal range before making any other adjustment in a treatment or correction?

3. What are video black and video white?

4. What is gamma?

5. How are RGB gain controls adjusted to create a sepia tone?

6. What is the Safe Color Limiter effect designed to prevent?

7. What is the major difference in the way automatic corrections are applied in the HSL group and the Curves group?

8. How can the Remove Color Cast tool improve the result of an automatic correction?

Lesson 5 Keyboard Shortcut

Key	Shortcut
Ctrl+Z (Windows)/Command+Z (Mac)	Undo

Color Treatments and Corrections

Now it is time for you to apply what you've learned and use the Color Effect to create color treatments for some shots from the episode. You'll also use the Color Correction auto corrections to better match between two cameras in a scene from the episode.

Media Used:

Hell's Kitchen

Duration:

15 to 20 minutes

GOALS

- Use the Color Effect to create a series of color treatments

- Use automatic color correction to create a series of color corrections

The Exercise 05 sequence contains a number of shots that require either treatment or correction.

- The first half of the sequence contains the shots the producer wants to be treated.

- The second half contains the scene with the non-unmatched cameras.

For the first half, the markers on each clip will tell you the look the producer wants. Experiment with the Color Effect to achieve the desired look.

For the second half, which is separated from the first by a black section, use the Color Correction auto corrections to make the shots match more closely. We aren't expecting perfection as this is only the offline edit, but the producer finds the difference between the cameras to be jarring, even at this stage of the edit.

Feel free to experiment and try different things as you work on the shots.

Nesting Multiple Effects

Until now we've applied no more than one effect to a given clip. There are times when more than one effect is required, however. For example, perhaps you want to apply a treatment to a shot and also blow it up. Media Composer allows you to do this via a process called *nesting*.

Media Used: Running the Sahara

Duration: 30 minutes

GOALS

- Apply more than one effect to a clip
- Change the order of nested effects

Nesting Effects

As you've learned previously, effects can be placed on any clip in the Timeline. But if an effect is already applied to that clip, the new effect replaces the existing effect. This is fine when you are experimenting to see which type of effect works best. But what if, for example, you want to both resize a clip and desaturate it?

Avid Media Composer allows you to apply multiple effects to a single clip via a process known as *nesting*. At the most basic level, a nest contains multiple effects on a single video segment. Nests, however, can be much more complex, with multiple layers all nested within a single clip.

In this lesson we'll look at simpler forms of nests, and in the next lesson we'll look at multilayer nests as part of our discussion of layering.

Let's load the sequence we'll be working with in this lesson.

To load the lesson sequence:

1. If the Running the Sahara project is not open from the last lesson, start Media Composer, select the **RUNNING THE SAHARA** project on the left side of the Open Project dialog box, and click the **OPEN** button.

   The Project window opens and lists all the bins associated with this project. The bin you'll use in this lesson is the RTS PT2 FX Sequences bin, which contains a number of sequences you'll use throughout this book.

2. Double-click the **RTS PT2 FX SEQUENCES** bin in the Project window to open it.

   We'd like to create a freeze frame of a clip already edited into the sequence, and fortunately that's very easy to do.

3. In the RTS PT2 FX Sequences bin window, double-click the **RTS FX PT2 LESSON 06** sequence. The sequence appears in the Record monitor.

Autonesting

If you need to apply more than one effect to a clip, the easiest approach is to use a technique known as *Autonesting*. This technique adds a new effect on top of an existing effect, such as a Resize effect on top of a Color Correction effect.

To load the first clip we want to work on:

1. Choose **TOOLS > MARKERS** to open the Markers window.

2. Double-click on the marker named **FIX ASPECT RATIO** to jump to that location in the Timeline.

Notice that this shot has a color correction already applied to it. In addition, it has been letterboxed, and there's a timecode readout burned into the frame over the upper letterbox region. This clip was obviously designed to be displayed in a standard 4×3 aspect ratio rather than the 16×9 aspect ratio of all other clips. As a result, it doesn't match anything else in the sequence, and the material inside the clip is distorted. We can correct this by resizing the clip vertically until the black bars are outside of the visible frame and the aspect ratio has been corrected.

We don't want to lose the correction, though, which is what would happen if we were to just drag and drop the Resize effect onto the clip.

To Autonest one effect on top of another:

1. Choose **Tools > Effect Palette** to open the Effect Palette.

2. Click on the **Image** category on the left side of the window. (See Figure 6.1.)

Figure 6.1
Image effects category.

3. Hold the **Alt** key (Windows) or **Option** key (Mac) down and apply the **Resize** effect to the clip.

The effect icon changes, and instead of a Color Correction effect icon we see a Resize effect icon. If you held the Alt key (Windows) or Option key (Mac) down throughout the entire drag-and-drop operation, the Resize effect was Autonested on top of the Color Correction effect, and the system should be showing the composited result of both effects. (The Resize effect, however, isn't actually doing anything yet. We'll modify its parameters in a moment.)

If, however, you saw the shot of the man in the turban change its appearance (with the beard becoming grayer and the shadows in the turban less well defined), then you didn't hold the Alt key (Windows) or Option key (Mac) key down through the entire drag-and-drop action. You'll need to undo your action and redo step 3, making sure that you hold the Alt key (Windows) or Option key (Mac) down until after you release the mouse.

You could continue to Autonest additional effects on top. This can be very beneficial, especially in advanced effects operations where you need to apply multiple treatments to a clip using, for example, both a Color Correction effect or a Color Effect and third-party plug-in effects. (Third-party plug-in effects are discussed in Appendix A, "Using AVX Third-Party Plug-ins.")

Other than the image appearing to still be color corrected, how can you tell that two effects are applied to the shot? You can use the Effect Editor, or you can display the nest in the Timeline. Let's look at each of those approaches.

Seeing Multiple Effects in the Effect Editor

If you have nested multiple effects on a single clip, the parameters for every effect applied are available in the Effect Editor.

To see and manipulate nested effects in the Effect Editor:

1. If you aren't already, park on the clip on which you Autonested the Resize effect.

2. Click on the **EFFECT MODE** button in the Timeline palette to enter Effect mode. (See Figure 6.2.) Notice that the Effect Editor shows both the Resize and Color Correction effects.

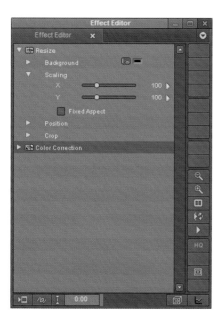

Figure 6.2
Effect Editor with two effects displayed.

While we're here, let's adjust the settings of the Resize effect to fix the shot's problem.

To convert a 16×9 letterboxed clip to a 16×9 widescreen clip:

1. If it isn't already, open the **SCALING** parameter group by clicking on the right-pointing triangle to the left of the group name.

2. Click on the **Y** parameter control and set the parameter to **133**, as shown in Figure 6.3. The black bars are no longer visible, and the image's distortion has been corrected.

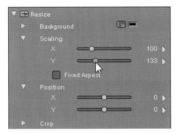

Figure 6.3
Position Y set to 133.

3. Scrub or play through the clip to see the finished effect.

Tip: If you know the specific value you want to use for an effect parameter, you can enter that value using the numbers on your keyboard. Simply click the parameter slider to activate it, and then type the desired value.

Displaying a Nest in the Timeline

The second way you can see effects within a nest is to display the nest in the Timeline. Two methods are available: simple nesting and expanded nesting.

Method One: Simple Nesting

In this method you travel down inside a nest, and the video Track monitor travels with you, allowing you to see the lower effects in isolation from the effects above them. This is a very useful technique, especially for complex effect nests, as it allows you to "lift up" higher effects so that you can focus on the effects beneath.

To step into an effect nest:

1. If you aren't already there, park the position indicator on the clip in the Timeline to which you just added the Resize effect.

2. Make sure that the **V1** track is active.

3. Click the **STEP IN** button at the bottom of the Timeline. (See Figure 6.4.)

Figure 6.4
Step In button.

Once you step into a nest, the Timeline view changes, and only the contents of the nest (i.e., what's beneath the Resize effect) are visible, as shown in Figure 6.5.

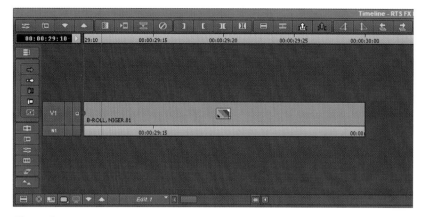

Figure 6.5
Resize effect nest contents.

When you are inside a nest, you can access only the contents of that nest. This means that not only are the clips before and after the effect you stepped into not accessible while you are inside the nest, but neither is audio.

We can continue to step in as long as there are effects to step into.

4. Click the **STEP IN** button again to step into the Color Correction effect to see the contents of that effect. (See Figure 6.6.)

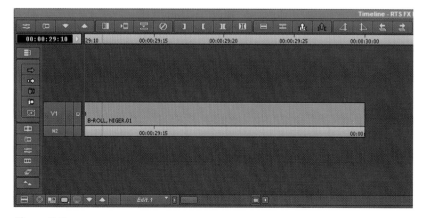

Figure 6.6
Color Correction effect nest contents.

Since there are no additional effects, the content of the Color Correction effect is the original clip. When you have stepped into a nest, you can always tell how deep you are by looking at the track patching panel. Beneath the video tracks appears a nest depth indicator, as shown in Figure 6.7.

Figure 6.7
Nest depth indicator.

In this case we are at nest level two, or two levels deep. The first nest level is inside the Resize effect, and the second level (where we are currently) is inside Color Correction effect. Effects are always processed from the bottom of the nest up. In this case, that means that Color Correction effect is processed, and then the results of the correction are fed into the Resize effect. This order of processing is significant and can have an impact on the final effect, as we'll see shortly.

Let's step back out to the top of the sequence.

To step out of an effect nest:

1. Click the **STEP OUT** button at the bottom of the Timeline. (See Figure 6.8.)

Figure 6.8
Step Out button.

You are now back to nest level one, above the Color Correction effect but below the Resize effect. Let's step out to the top of the nest.

2. Click the **STEP OUT** button once more to step out of the nest.

Now let's look at the other method of stepping into a nest, expanded nesting.

Method Two: Expanded Nesting

Compared to simple nesting, expanded nesting lets you see the sequence and the nest contents simultaneously. It also allows you to listen to audio and access all material in the sequence before and after the effect nest you are working with.

In addition, as opposed to simple nesting, the video monitor is always positioned at the top of the nest and cannot travel into the nest. As a result, with expanded nesting you are able to edit the contents of a nest but still see the composite of all effects within the nest.

Let's step into the same Resize effect nest as before, using expanded nesting.

To step into an effect nest:

1. If you aren't already there, park the position indicator on the clip in the Timeline to which you just added the Resize effect.

2. Make sure that the **V1** track is active.

3. Alt-click (Windows) or Option-click (Mac) the **Step In** button at the bottom of the Timeline. The Timeline displays the tracks inside and outside the nest, with the tracks inside the nest appearing directly above the track that contains the nest, as shown in Figure 6.9.

Figure 6.9
Expanded nesting.

Tip: You can also enter and exit expanded nesting by double-clicking a high-lighted segment. This can be disabled via the Timeline setting.

4. Now let's step in once more. Alt-click (Windows) or Option-click (Mac) the **Step In** button at the bottom of the Timeline again. The Timeline displays both levels of the nest, as shown in Figure 6.10.

Figure 6.10
Expanded nesting showing both levels of the nest.

As with simple nesting, the Track panel indicates the nest level for each element within the nest, this time using two numbers separated by a period instead of just one. (See Figure 6.11.)

Figure 6.11
Expanded nesting track indicators.

The first number indicates the nest level of the track. The number 1 indicates the track is on the first level of the nest, and the number 2 indicates that you are stepped in twice (the source of an effect within an effect).

The second number indicates the track number at that layer of the nest (i.e., video track 1 at that nest layer, video track 2 at that nest layer, and so on).

In addition, each level of the nest is assigned a different track color to help differentiate it from other nest levels.

Changing the Order of Nested Effects

Although it isn't the case for all effect combinations, there are times when the order of the effects in the nest is important. If the effects are in the wrong order, in some cases you'll get the wrong result. The Resize effect is one of those effects whose position in the nest can be significant.

Let's experiment with the very last clip in the sequence and see what it would look like if presented in a "cinema widescreen" aspect ratio of 2.39:1. To do this we will add a special masking effect to mask off the portions of the frame that wouldn't be visible in that wider aspect ratio.

To add a film widescreen mask to a shot:

1. Choose **TOOLS > MARKERS** to open the Markers window.

2. Double-click on the **LETTERBOX** marker to jump to that location in the Timeline.

3. If it isn't already open, press **CTRL+8** (Windows) or **COMMAND+8** (Mac) to open the Effect Palette.

4. Click on the **IMAGE** effects category on the left side of the window.

5. Select the **Mask** effect (Figure 6.12) and drag it to the **Runners, Out of the Sun** clip at the end of the sequence.

Figure 6.12
Mask effect.

Similar to the Color Effect, Mask has no effect by default. You can manipulate the effect parameters to mask off regions of the frame either vertically or horizontally.

6. Click on the **Effect Mode** button in the Timeline tool palette to enter Effect mode. The parameters for the Mask effect are displayed in the Effect Editor, as shown in Figure 6.13. The Scaling parameter group is used to add a colored mask over the frame.

Figure 6.13
Mask effect parameters.

7. Set the **Height** parameter to **74**. We've done the math for you, and the resulting mask provides a 2.39:1 aspect ratio within the masked area.

8. Scrub through the shot to see the results of the effect.

The shot looks good, but the producer suggests that it would look better if the runners were a bit lower in the frame. We can accomplish this using a Resize effect, which includes parameters that let us move the image within the video frame.

To move the image down in the frame:

1. Hold down the **ALT** (Windows) or **OPTION** (Mac) key down and drag the **RESIZE** effect (Image category) from the Effect Palette to the last clip in the Timeline. Recall that holding the Alt (Windows) or Option (Mac) key down while applying an effect will Autonest that effect on top of the existing effect rather than replacing it.

2. If necessary, re-enter Effect mode.

3. Open the **POSITION** parameter group in the Effect Editor (see Figure 6.14).

Figure 6.14
Resize effect, Position parameter.

4. Set the **Y** parameter in the **POSITION** group to **50** to move the runners down in the frame.

Wait a moment. Take a look at the result of that parameter change. Though the runners are now positioned lower in the frame, the mask moved downward as well. (See Figure 6.15.) Why did that happen?

Figure 6.15
Effect results.

When more than one effect is applied to a clip, the effects are processed one at a time, from the bottom of the nest to the top. Not only that, but for basic effects, the composited result of each effect is fed up to the next effect in the nest. In this effect nest, that means that the Mask effect is applied to the original clip, and then the mask plus the clip (the result of the applied effect) is passed to the Resize effect for processing.

As you can tell, this isn't what we want. We want the mask to stay in the position we gave it and the shot to move inside the mask. To accomplish this, we need the Resize effect to be applied *before* the Mask effect. Fortunately this is very easy to accomplish in the Effect Editor.

To reorder effects in a nest:

1. If necessary, park on the last clip in the sequence and enter Effect mode. The Effect Editor appears, as shown in Figure 6.16.

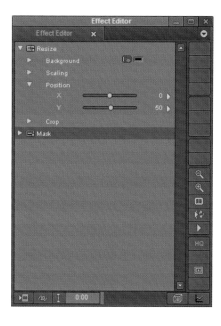

Figure 6.16
Effect Editor showing the nested effects.

Recall that both of the effects in the nest are visible in the Effect Editor. The Resize effect is displayed first, then the Mask effect below it. This is always the case with nested effects. The bottom-most effect in the Effect Editor is at the bottom of the nest, and then all other effects are listed, traveling upward, in the order they are applied. To reorder effects in the nest, we simply drag and drop the effects to change their position in the nest.

2. Click on the **RESIZE** effect icon in the Effect Editor and drag it downward until it is below the Mask effect, then release the mouse button. (See Figure 6.17.) Remember that an effect's icon is always just to the left of the effect name.

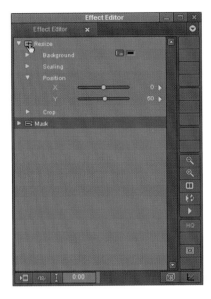

Figure 6.17
Resize effect icon in the Effect Editor.

The effects are reordered in the Effect Editor, as shown in Figure 6.18, and the result is now correct, with the Resize effect being applied only to the shot and not to the shot and the mask. (See Figure 6.19.)

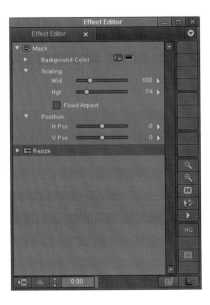

Figure 6.18
Effects reordered in the Effect Editor.

Figure 6.19
Effect results.

For the most part, effects that can be nested can also be reordered. There are some exceptions to this, and the system will display a dialog box explaining why when you encounter an exception.

Review/Discussion Questions

1. How do you add an effect to a clip in the Timeline on top of an existing effect?

2. What is that procedure called?

3. What are the two different methods you can use to view the effects inside of a nest?

4. What is an advantage of simple nesting?

5. What is an advantage of expanded nesting?

6. How do you change the order of effects within a nest?

7. What effect can be used to letterbox a clip?

Lesson 6   Keyboard Shortcut

Key	Shortcut
Ctrl+8 (Windows)/Command+8 (Mac)	**Open Effect Palette**

Nesting and Order of Processing

In this exercise, you're going to look at how order of processing can affect effect results. You'll also learn how you can take advantage of this order of processing to get better results.

Media Used:
Running the Sahara

Duration:
15 minutes

GOALS

- Apply more than one effect to a clip in the sequence
- Learn how the order of effect processing can affect the final result

The first two cuts in the sequence are of the same clip. This clip requires both an automatic Color Correction effect and a Resize effect to eliminate the letterbox. To see how order of processing affects results, apply the effects in the following order:

■ First clip: Apply the automatic Color Correction effect first and the Resize effect second.

■ Second clip: Apply the Resize effect first and the automatic Color Correction effect second.

Why are the results different? Because in the letterboxed region, both the burn-in and the bars affected the contrast range that the automatic correction saw. Eliminating those bars makes for a more-accurate correction.

On the third clip, apply the following effects:

■ Flop

■ Resize (to zoom in tighter on the sun)

■ Color Effect (to create a desaturated treatment)

On the fourth clip, apply the following effects:

■ Timewarp (to slow the shot down to create a "dreamy" look)

■ Color Correction (to open up the contrast and brighten the shot)

■ Color Effect (to desaturate the colors)

Feel free to experiment and try different things as you work on the shots. Try also changing the order of effect application. How does changing the order affect the result? Are there any effects in this exercise that cannot be applied on top of another effect?

Multilayer Effects

Until now, we've added effects to video clips on a single track of video. But that will only take you so far. Many effects require multiple tracks of video, with effects that combine, or *composite*, them together into a single image. In this lesson, you will learn how to start building multilayer effects in Media Composer.

Media Used: **Running the Sahara**

Duration: **60 minutes**

GOALS

- Layer using video tracks
- Use the Picture-in-Picture effect
- Reorder effect layers
- Create keyframe effects using keyframe graphs
- Use reformatting effects
- Explore how nesting interacts with layering

Creating Multilayer Effects

Sometimes more than one video clip needs to play at once. For example, you may want to have an interview in the corner of the frame overlaid on video of the subject being discussed. You might want to blend two or more clips using chroma keys or other effects. It may even be as simple as superimposing a title over video.

All of these are examples of multilayer effects. The most common multilayer effects can be found in the Blend category of the Effect Palette and include Superimpose and Picture-in-Picture. There are many third-party plug-in effects that allow you to create more elaborate composites and effects.

In this lesson we'll cover the basics of how to build multilayer effects and look at an advanced method of keyframing that is especially useful when animating the position of these effects. Let's start with some of the fundamental techniques you use when creating and editing multilayer effects.

To load the lesson sequence:

1. If the Running the Sahara project is not open from the previous lesson, open Media Composer, select the **RUNNING THE SAHARA** project on the left side of the Open Project dialog box, and click the **OPEN** button.

   The Project window opens and lists all the bins associated with this project. The bin you'll use in this lesson is the 1 RTS PT2 FX Sequences bin, which contains a number of sequences you'll use throughout this book.

2. Double-click the **1 RTS PT2 FX SEQUENCES** bin in the Project window to open it.

   We'd like to create a freeze frame of a clip already edited into the sequence, and that's very easy to do.

3. In the 1 RTS PT2 FX Sequences bin window, double-click the **RTS FX PT2 LESSON 07A** sequence. The sequence appears in the Record monitor.

Creating a Picture-in-Picture Effect

A Picture-in-Picture (PIP) effect is one of the most commonly used multilayer effects. A PIP allows you to layer one clip over another and adjust the size, position, and opacity of the upper clip. The first clip in the lesson sequence shows three runners in a sand storm. Let's add a PIP in the upper corner of the frame of one of the runners talking about the experience.

To add a PIP above the first clip:

1. Mark the first clip, **RUNNERS, SAND,** in the Timeline and press **T** on the keyboard to mark the clip's duration. Now let's find the source interview we'd like to use.

2. Locate the Project window and open the **2 RTS SOURCE CLIPS** bin.

3. Double-click on the **RUNNER 1, INT** clip to load it into the Source monitor.

4. With the Source monitor active, move to timecode **15:10:07:11** and mark an IN.

Note: Don't worry that the audio is missing. We are focused on the video effects in this module, and getting the audio edit right is not important right now.

This PIP needs to go on its own video track above the first clip.

5. In the Timeline, click on the **V1** source track in the patching panel and drag it to the V2 sequence track, as shown in Figure 7.1, to patch the source to video track 2.

Figure 7.1
Patch source to sequence track V2.

6. Click the **OVERWRITE EDIT** button between the two monitors in the Composer window or press **B** on the keyboard to overwrite the interview clip onto V2.

7. Choose **TOOLS > EFFECT PALETTE** to open the Effect Palette.

8. Select the **BLEND** category from the left side of the palette and drag the **PICTURE-IN-PICTURE** effect (see Figure 7.2) to the new clip on V2.

Figure 7.2
Blend effects category.

The effect is applied and resizes the clip on V2 by 50%, centering it in the frame. This is the default configuration of the Picture-in-Picture effect, but it isn't what we want. Let's take a look at the parameters available in this effect.

Configuring the Picture-in-Picture Effect

Take a look at the Record monitor in the Composer window. Notice that there appears to be a faint black line all around the PIP effect. (See Figure 7.3.) That wasn't caused by the effect, but rather is what is known as *blanking*. Blanking almost always exists on standard-definition video and is sometimes visible on high-definition video, depending on the type of camera used. We want to remove this blanking so it is not visible, and we can use the Crop parameter to do so.

Figure 7.3
Blanking visible at edges of PIP effect.

In this case the blanking is relatively similar on all sides, and we can do a simple crop adjustment to remove it.

To crop the blanking from the edges of the frame:

1. Enter Effect mode. The Effect Editor opens, showing the parameters available for the PIP effect.

2. Open the **Crop** parameter group to see its parameters. (See Figure 7.4.)

   The Crop parameters adjust between 0 and positive or negative 999. A movement either down or to the right is a positive movement, and up or to the left is a negative movement.

Figure 7.4
PIP effect, Crop parameters.

3. Set the **Top** crop to **10**.

4. Set the **Bot** (bottom) crop to **-10**.

5. Set the **Lft** (left) crop to **10**.

6. Set the **Rgt** (right) crop to **-10**.

The blanking is now cropped out of the frame, as shown in Figure 7.5.

Figure 7.5
Blanking cropped from
edges of PIP effect.

Tip: Cropping can also be used to change the aspect ratio of an image being composited onto another. For example, you could create a "portrait" image by cropping out a large amount of the frame on the left and right or a wider aspect ratio by cropping off the top and the bottom.

Now let's set the position and the size of the PIP. The default position and size aren't really appropriate for this effect.

To change the position and size of the PIP:

1. In the Effect Editor, open the **Scaling** and **Position** parameter groups, as shown in Figure 7.6.

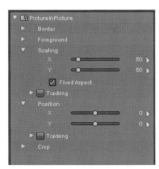

Figure 7.6
Scaling and Position parameter groups.

2. Set the **Scaling X** and **Y** parameters to **33**.

The Position parameters can be set to values between –999 and 999, with 0 being the center of the screen. Positive values represent positions down or to the right of the center, while negative values represent positions up or to the left of the center. Let's position the PIP in the upper-left region of the screen.

3. Set the **POSITION X** parameter to **–225**.

4. Set the **POSITION Y** parameter to **–225**.

Your effect should look like that shown in Figure 7.7.

Figure 7.7
PIP effect in position.

5. Play or scrub through the effect to see how it looks so far.

Animating the Picture-in-Picture Effect

The effect looks good, but we need to consider how the PIP will begin and end. Currently it simply pops on and pops off with our clip. That may be fine, but instead let's have the PIP move on from the left edge at the beginning and fade out at the end. To create this motion we will need to create two keyframes for each transition, one to start it and one to end it.

To move the PIP onscreen at the beginning:

1. Move to 15 frames into the effect and press the **APOSTROPHE** (') key on the keyboard to add a keyframe. This first keyframe "holds" the current position and is where we want the motion to "land."

2. Move to the beginning of the effect and add another keyframe.

3. Drag the **POSITION X** slider to the left until the PIP is just off screen and no longer visible.

4. Play or scrub through the effect to see the result so far.

Now let's fade out the PIP at the end. We will use the Foreground parameter to do this.

To fade out the PIP at the end:

1. Move to one second before the end of the effect and add a keyframe.

Tip: To accomplish this quickly, you can move to the end of the effect and type –100 on the numeric keypad to move back one second.

2. Move to the end of the effect and add another keyframe.

3. In the Effect Editor, open the **FOREGROUND** parameter group.

4. Set the **LEVEL** parameter to **0** (zero).

5. Play through the completed effect.

Creating a "Card Swap" Multilayer Transition

Now let's build a slightly more complex multilayer effect. In this case, we want to use what is sometimes referred to as a "card swap" to move from one shot to the next. The two shots in the Timeline take place in different locales and times, and we'd like to use the effect to help the audience understand that we're changing locations.

The card swap transition requires that both shots be onscreen at the same time during the transition, which implies that one is layered on top of the other. But we have a straight cut in the Timeline. To build our effect we first need to create an overlap of the two shots. There are a number of ways we can do this, but let's use the Match Frame command to help us extend the first shot over the second.

To set up the clips for the effect:

1. Park on the last frame of the **MAUR, RUNNERS PLANNING** clip.

Tip: A quick way to park on the last frame of a clip is to hold down the Ctrl+Alt (Windows) or Command+Option (Mac) keys and click near the end of a clip. The position indicator will automatically snap to the clip's last frame.

2. Select **MATCH FRAME** from the Composer window **FAST** menu.

The clip is loaded into the Source monitor, and an IN point is marked at the matched frame. This isn't the correct frame, though. We need to mark an IN at the *next* frame in the clip. Otherwise we'll have a duplicate frame as the first frame in our effect.

3. Press the **RIGHT ARROW** key on the keyboard once to advance one frame and then mark an IN.

4. Type **+129** on the numeric keyboard to advance the position indicator and then mark an OUT to mark a two-second duration.

5. If necessary, patch from V1 in the source to V2 in the sequence and ensure that V2 in the sequence is enabled and V1 in the sequence is disabled.

Note: **You should still be properly configured from the last effect, but if you've quit and restarted since then, you may no longer be set up correctly.**

6. Ctrl-click (Windows) or Command-click (Mac) on the **Maur, Runners 2, Night** clip to snap to the first frame of that clip.

7. Overwrite the source clip onto V2 on top of the beginning of the third clip.

   We're almost finished. All we need to do is break the Maur, Runners 2, Night clip into two parts: the part below the other clip, and the remainder of the clip.

8. Ctrl-click (Windows) or Command-click (Mac) on the region of the **Maur, Runners 2, Night** clip that is just past the edit you made to select the first frame after the clip on V2.

Now the transition is set up correctly and should look like Figure 7.8.

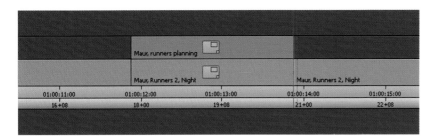

Figure 7.8
Clips edited in for Card Cut transition.

Building the Effect

Now let's build the effect for one of the two clips. We'll start with the clip on top, which in this case is the outgoing clip. This clip should shrink down in size and into one of the corners of the frame. Then, after sitting in that position for a second, it should fly out to the corner it is positioned near.

To animate the outgoing clip:

1. Apply a PIP effect to the **Maur, runners planning** clip on V2 and enter Effect mode. Notice that this clip has the same visible blanking as the clip we applied the PIP to previously. We can use the same cropping technique as before.

2. Set the TOP crop to **10**.

3. Set the BOT (bottom) crop to **–10**.

4. Set the LFT (left) crop to 10.

5. Set the RGT (right) crop to **–10**. The blanking is now cropped out of the frame.

6. Park on the first frame of the effect and add a keyframe. This keyframe sets the starting position of the effect.

7. Type **+15** on the numeric keyboard and press ENTER (Windows) or RETURN (Mac) to advance the position indicator by half a second.

8. Add a keyframe at this position.

9. Set the SCALING X and Y parameters to **40**.

10. Set the POSITION X and Y parameters to **–200**.

11. Type **+30** on the numeric keyboard and press ENTER (Windows) or RETURN (Mac) to advance the position indicator by a second.

12. Add a keyframe at this position to set the start of the animation that will take the clip out of the frame.

13. Move to the last frame of the effect and add a final keyframe.

14. Set the POSITION X and Y parameters to **–700**.

15. Play through the effect to see the outgoing clip animation.

The outgoing clip's animation looks great, and now we need to create a similar animation for the incoming clip. Instead of shrinking to a corner and then flying out, it has the opposite animation, flying in (from a different corner) and then blowing up to full screen. Since the two animations are so similar, we can use the outgoing clip's effect as the foundation for the incoming clip.

To animate the incoming clip:

1. Click on the icon in the upper-left corner of the Effect Editor to "grab" the effect and drag it onto the lower of the two clips in the transition stack.

2. Scrub through the clip and notice that you can't even see the lower clip. That's because it has identical animation to the upper clip. We need its animation to be the reverse of the upper clip. Many effects in Media Composer contain a Reverse Animation parameter that will swap the order of all keyframes within the effect. In the Picture-in-Picture effect this parameter is found within the Foreground parameter group, as shown in Figure 7.9.

Figure 7.9
Reverse Animation parameter.

3. If necessary, select the **PIP** effect on the lower of the two clips.

4. Open the **FOREGROUND** parameter group and enable the **REVERSE ANIMATION** parameter to reverse the animation keyframes.

5. Scrub through the clip. Notice that although the animation is reversed, the incoming clip has the same positioning as the outgoing clip. We need to change the Position values so that it flies in from and rests inside the opposite corner of the frame.

6. Click on the first keyframe in the effect to select it.

7. Set the **POSITION X** and **Y** parameters to **700**.

8. Now select the middle two keyframes by clicking on the second keyframe and then Shift-clicking on the third.

9. Set the **POSITION X** and **Y** parameters to **200**.

10. Scrub through the effect to see the finished result.

The effect looks good, but the black background is a little stark. It might look better if we had a background clip play beneath the transition.

To add a background clip to the Card Cut transition:

1. Choose **CLIP > NEW VIDEO TRACK** or press **CTRL+Y** (Windows) or **COMMAND+Y** (Mac) to add a third video track.

2. Select the **SEGMENT LIFT/OVERWRITE** mode from the Timeline Smart palette. (See Figure 7.10.)

Figure 7.10
Segment Lift/Overwrite.

The Segment Lift/Overwrite tool is extremely useful in effect design. It can be used to move effect segments from track to track without affecting sync downstream.

3. Click on the lower of the two clips in the sequence and, Ctrl+Shift-drag (Windows) or Control+Shift-drag (Mac) the clip up to V3 as shown in Figure 7.11. Do not release the keyboard modifiers until after you release the mouse button.

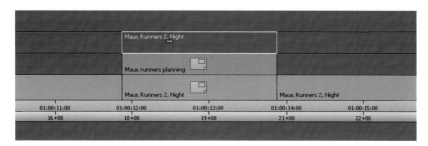

Figure 7.11
Moving the clip on V1 to V3.

You should now have an empty space below the two clips.

4. Park in the middle of the effect stack and press **T** on the keyboard to mark the duration of the effect stack.

5. Locate the Project window and open the **2 RTS SOURCE CLIPS** bin.

6. Double-click on the **SAND 3** clip to load it into the Source monitor.

7. Use the Timeline Patch panel to patch the source clip to V1 in the sequence. Make sure that V2 and V3 are both disabled.

8. Park at the first frame of the **SAND 3** clip and press the **B** key on the keyboard to overwrite the source clip into the marked hole on V1. The sequence should now look like Figure 7.12.

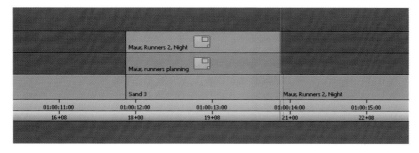

Figure 7.12
Final Card Cut transition effect stack.

9. Play through the effect to see the final version.

Advanced Keyframing Using Graphs

Keyframing in the Composer window is convenient but limited. In the Effect Editor, you have the tools to create complex effect animations. This section will introduce you to the basics of animating your effects using keyframe graphs.

Keyframe graphs enable you to see graphically the change in parameter values over time for every parameter in an effect. With the exception of "switch" parameters such as the Reverse Animation parameter, each parameter has its own keyframe graph. Let's take a look at the parameter graphs for one of the effects we just created.

To display keyframe graphs:

1. Park on the **Card Cut** transition effect stack and enter Effect mode.

2. Click on the effect on V3 to display the parameters of that effect.

3. Click the **Show/Hide Keyframe Graphs** button (see Figure 7.13) to expand the Effect Editor to show the keyframe graphs.

Figure 7.13
Show/Hide Keyframe Graphs.

The keyframe graphs for the incoming clip's animation are displayed. (See Figure 7.14.)

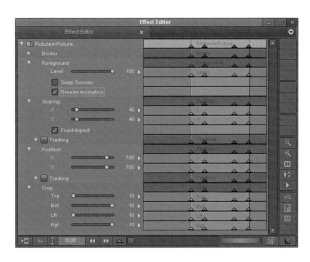

Figure 7.14
Incoming effect's keyframe graph.

Note that every parameter contains four keyframes. That's because we created those keyframes from the Record monitor. Most of them aren't really necessary and can get in the way when editing with graphs. Fortunately, the system provides a simple mechanism for removing them.

To remove redundant keyframes:

1. Right-click on the yellow region at the top of the keyframe graphs and choose **Remove Redundant Keyframes** from the pop-up menu, as shown in Figure 7.15.

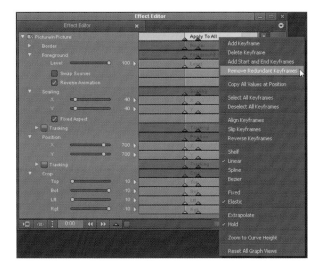

Figure 7.15
Removing redundant keyframes.

The redundant (unnecessary) keyframes are removed, leaving only those keyframes required for the animation you created. (See Figure 7.16.)

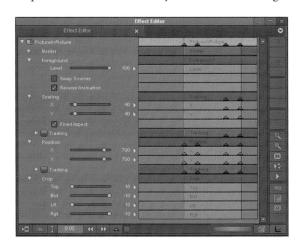

Figure 7.16
Required keyframes for effect.

Notice that there are no keyframes for any of the Crop parameters, even though we cropped out the blanking with them. If a parameter has only a single value for the duration of the effect, a keyframe is not necessary. Keyframes are required only when a parameter's value is changing over time.

Adding Keyframes from the Keyframe Graphs

As keyframes can be applied independently to each parameter, many different results are possible when you click the Add Keyframe button. Before the keyframe can be added, the Avid system must be told how to add the keyframe. The following methods are provided:

- **Add Keyframes to Active Parameter.** Adds keyframes only to the active, or selected, parameter. As only one parameter can be active at any given time, this option affects only a single parameter. A parameter group must be open and a parameter selected or no keyframe will be added.

- **Add Keyframes to Active Group.** Adds keyframes to all parameters in the active group. If a parameter is selected in a group, keyframes are added to all parameters within that group. A parameter group must be open and a parameter selected or no keyframes will be added.

- **Add Keyframes to Open Groups.** Adds keyframes to all parameters in all open parameter groups. At least one group must be open, or no keyframes will be added.

- **Add Keyframes to Enabled Groups.** Adds keyframes to all parameters in all enabled parameter groups. The groups can be either opened or closed. At least one parameter group must be enabled, or no keyframes will be added.

- **Add Keyframes to Open Graphs.** Adds keyframes to all parameters that have their keyframe graphs displayed. At least one keyframe graph must be open, or no keyframes will be added.

- **Add Keyframes to All Parameters.** Adds keyframes to every parameter in the effect.

To select the keyframe addition method:

1. Right-click the Add Keyframe button at the bottom of the Effect Editor.

2. Choose the desired option from the list at the bottom of the menu. (See Figure 7.17.)

Figure 7.17
Add Keyframe options.

Now let's go one step further. When you open the keyframe graphs area, you don't see just the keyframes for each parameter. You can also display a graph for each parameter, showing the change in parameter value over time. These graphs are displayed using the arrow next to each keyframe region. Let's take a look at the keyframe graphs for the Position parameters.

To display a parameter's keyframe graph:

1. Click the arrow next to the **POSITION X** parameter to display its keyframe graph.

2. Click the arrow next to the **POSITION Y** parameter to display its keyframe graph as well.

3. Scroll downward in the Effect Editor so you can see both graphs. The Effect Editor now shows both keyframe graphs, as shown in Figure 7.18.

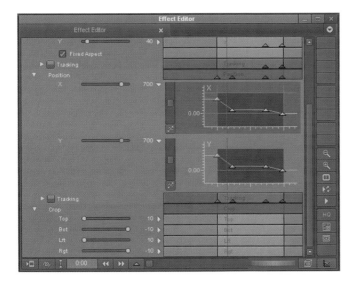

Figure 7.18
Position parameter keyframe graphs.

The graphs are a bit small, relative to the available area. Media Composer allows us to resize the graphs vertically using either a Vertical Height slider or a Zoom to Curve Height button. (See Figure 7.19.)

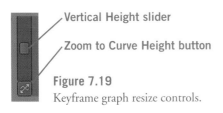

Vertical Height slider

Zoom to Curve Height button

Figure 7.19
Keyframe graph resize controls.

4. Click the **ZOOM TO CURVE HEIGHT** button for both the Position X and Position Y keyframe graphs. The graphs are resized based on parameter values, so that the graph is as tall as possible, as shown in Figure 7.20.

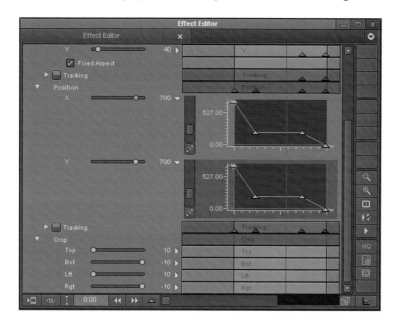

Figure 7.20
Resized Position parameter keyframe graphs.

Tip: You can make a keyframe graph even taller by clicking and dragging from the bottom.

Keyframe Interpolation Options

Just as was the case with Timewarp keyframes, effect keyframes support four methods of interpolation: linear, spline, Bézier, and shelf.

■ A linear keyframe creates a direct path between two keyframe values. *Linear* means that the rate of change is continuous between the two keyframes, and there is no gradual acceleration (ease-in) or deceleration (ease-out) from one keyframe to another.

■ Spline creates a path with natural ease-in and ease-out at every keyframe. The amount of ease-in and ease-out is automatically calculated to create a smooth transition into and out of keyframes and cannot be adjusted.

■ Bézier creates a path with natural ease-in and ease-out at every keyframe. Unlike spline interpolation, the shape of the animation curve can be adjusted on either side of the keyframe by manipulating the Bézier curve handles.

■ Shelf holds a keyframe's value until the next keyframe. This interpolation type is used to cause the parameter to jump instantly from one value to another.

In the Avid Learning Series

Learn more about the powerful keyframing tools available in Media Composer 6 by picking up the companion book in this series, *Media Composer 6: Advanced Effects and Compositing*.

By default, effect keyframes use linear interpolation. We can make the motion smoother if we switch to spline interpolation.

To switch the keyframe interpolation:

1. Right-click on the **POSITION X** keyframe graph and choose **SPLINE** from the pop-up menu. (See Figure 7.21.)

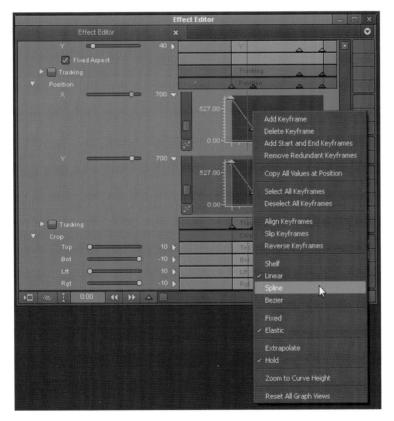

Figure 7.21
Spline keyframe interpolation.

2. Right-click on the **Position Y** keyframe graph and choose **Spline** from the pop-up menu. The keyframe's interpolation for both Position parameters has been changed to spline, as shown in Figure 7.22. Notice that the line between the keyframes is no longer linear but has a slight curvature heading into and out of each keyframe.

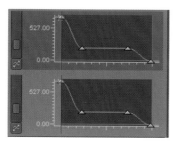

Figure 7.22
Spline interpolation of Position parameters.

3. If not already set, click the monitor next to V3 to monitor from that track.

4. Play through the effect to see the difference in the motion. The motion of the incoming and outgoing clips is a bit different now because one of them is set to linear and the other now set to spline. Let's set them both to spline so the motion matches once again.

5. Click on the **Incoming** effect on V2 to display its parameters in the Effect Editor. Notice that the Position keyframe graphs are open. That's because you opened the graphs for the Effect Editor, not just for a single effect.

6. If necessary, scroll down in the Effect Editor so both graphs are fully visible.

7. Right-click on the **Position X** keyframe graph and choose **Spline** from the pop-up menu.

8. Right-click on the **Position Y** keyframe graph and choose **Spline** from the pop-up menu.

9. Play through the effect to see the result.

Layers and Nests

As you may recall from the previous lesson, whenever you add an effect to a clip, you create a nest, and you can step into that nest and apply additional effects. It is even possible to add video tracks within a nest and create self-contained effects. This can be extremely useful as it allows you to do things such as add a title to the contents of a PIP and use the PIP effect parameters to animate both the clip and the title. Let's do that to add a lower-third title to the PIP we created at the beginning of the sequence.

To add a title to a PIP:

1. Move the position indicator to the first clip in the sequence.

2. If necessary, turn on track **V2**.

3. Click the **STEP IN** button at the bottom of the Timeline to step into the PIP. The contents of the nest are shown in Figure 7.23.

Figure 7.23
PIP effect nest contents.

Notice that this nest contains two tracks: an empty V1 and a V2 that contains the clip we applied the PIP to. That's because the PIP is a *two-input* effect. These two inputs are represented in the nest. The top track in the foreground input is the clip we applied the nest to. The bottom track represents the background and references the contents on the track (or tracks) beneath the PIP effect outside of the nest.

4. Click on the monitor next to V1 to show the background for the PIP effect. The shot of the three runners in the sandstorm is displayed. You should always leave the V1 track inside of the nest empty, as editing a clip into this track will replace the background within the effect.

5. Click on the monitor next to V2 to show the clip we applied the PIP to. Inside the nest we have the full editing capabilities of the system, including the ability to create additional video tracks.

6. Press **CTRL+Y** (Windows) or **COMMAND+Y** (Mac) to add a third video track.

7. Open the **RTS TITLES** bin and load the **TITLE: WA L3** title into the Source monitor. This title identifies the speaker on camera.

8. Click on the Timeline and press the **T** key on the keyboard to mark the nest duration.

9. Use the Timeline Patch panel to patch the source to V3 in the sequence.

10. Check to make sure that track V2 in the sequence is deselected.

11. Press the **B** key on the keyboard to overwrite the title onto V3. Your sequence should look like the Timeline shown in Figure 7.24.

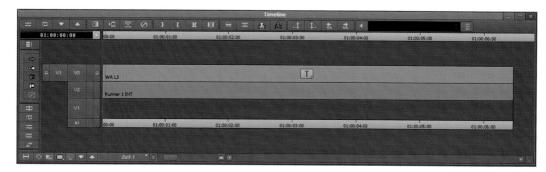

Figure 7.24
Title added to the PIP effect nest.

12. Click the **STEP OUT** button at the bottom of the Timeline to step out of the nest.

13. Play through the effect.

Notice that when you play the effect, the title moves in sync with the image inside the PIP. By placing the title inside the PIP we have essentially "grouped" it with the clip we applied the PIP to. We don't have to keyframe the title because it is also animated by the PIP's parameters.

Nesting Effects Within Titles

As we saw, a PIP has two tracks inside the nest. What about a title? Let's take a look inside a title nest.

To step into a title:

1. Move to the end of the sequence and park on the fourth clip in the Timeline (**MAUR, SUNSET**). A title with the name of the program has already been edited onto V2.

2. Click the **STEP IN** button at the bottom of the Timeline to step into the title's nest. The title's nest is shown in Figure 7.25.

   Title nests have three video tracks. V1 represents the background for the title, just as it did for PIP effects. V2 and V3 represent the two parts of the title: its fill (on V2) and its matte (on V3).

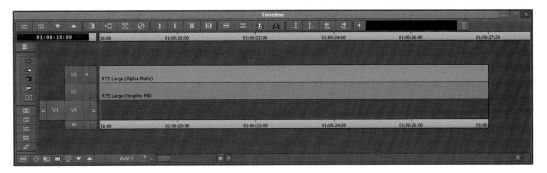

Figure 7.25
Nest contents of a title.

3. Click on the monitor for the V3 track. The matte is used to define the edges of the title and indicate where the title and the background are displayed. Black indicates where the title is displayed and white where the background is displayed. The title matte is locked and cannot be modified.

4. Click on the monitor for the V2 track.

The fill is what is displayed wherever the matte indicates that the title should be visible. By default it is the fill that was selected when the title was created. The fill can be modified or replaced if desired. Let's change the fill to a video clip—in this case, the same clip that is used for the background.

To replace the title fill:

1. Move to the first frame of the nest.

2. Select track **V1** and deselect all other tracks.

3. Choose **MATCH FRAME** from the Composer window **FAST** menu. The title background, in this case the **MAUR, SUNSET** clip, is loaded into the Source monitor.

4. Patch the source to V2 in the sequence.

5. Press **T** on the keyboard to mark the duration of the nest and then press **B** on the keyboard to overwrite the title fill with the **MAUR, SUNSET** clip. If we were to step out of the nest, the title would appear to be invisible as the same clip was used for both the background and the fill. Let's fix this by using the Color Effect to change the look of the fill.

6. Press **CTRL+8** (Windows) or **COMMAND+8** (Mac) to open the Effect Palette.

7. Select the **IMAGE** category and apply a **COLOR EFFECT** to the clip on V2.

8. Select EFFECT MODE from the Timeline tool palette.

9. Click on the INVERT parameter in the LUMA ADJUST parameter group.

10. Set the RED COLOR GAIN parameter to **125**.

11. Set the BLUE COLOR GAIN parameter to **50**.

12. Step out of the nest and scrub through the finished effect. The title is now much more effective than it would be with a simple color fill.

Deciding When to Layer or Nest

As we've seen, both layering and nesting are useful and powerful. But how do you decide whether to layer or nest? Use the following guidelines to help you decide.

- Layer to add an element to a multilayer effect design.

- Nest to add an element to another element or to modify only that element.

For example, to add a title as a new element in a multilayer effect design, you should layer. However, if you want to add the title within a Picture-in-Picture effect, nest the title into the PIP.

Applying Effects to Tracks

In addition to applying effects to clips, we can also apply them directly to tracks. Though this isn't useful for most effects, there are several types of clips for which this is extremely useful. One of these is the Safe Color Limiter, which we mentioned in Lesson 5, "Color Treating and Correcting." Applying effects to empty video tracks, known as applying effects to filler, is a unique feature to Avid editing systems and can be quite powerful.

Using the Safe Color Limiter

The limiter is most commonly applied to an upper-level video track so that it limits the entire Timeline. Alternatively, it can be applied only to selected regions of the Timeline using the Add Edit command to create edits in the filler track.

Let's apply the Safe Color Limiter effect to the filler region above the last clip in the Timeline.

To apply the Safe Color Limiter:

1. Park on the last clip in the Timeline. This clip has the night vision look we created in Lesson 5.

2. Open the Effect Palette and select the IMAGE category.

3. Select the SAFE COLOR LIMITER effect and drag to the **V2** track region directly above the RUNNER 1 NIGHT INT clip, as shown in Figure 7.26.

Figure 7.26
The Safe Color Limiter effect applied to the V2 filler above the clip.

Once applied, the limiter immediately restricts the signal output of everything beneath it. Let's compare the unlimited and limited versions of the Color Effect.

4. Move the cursor to the Track monitor region of the Timeline and click on the V2 monitor to move the monitor up to see the composite result of tracks V1 and V2. We are now looking at the limited output. Let's see what the limiter did.

5. Focus your attention on the campfire region of the frame and toggle the monitor between V1 and V2.

    Do you see how the fire's green is slightly muted by the limiter? That's because it has determined that the green output was too high and wasn't acceptable for broadcast. Nothing else in the scene is limited, as it is all within the acceptable signal boundaries.

The Safe Color Limiter effect can be applied as necessary to individual effects or multilayer effects in the Timeline, or it can be applied to an empty track above the entire sequence. When you apply it to the entire sequence, it means that everything in the sequence will be limited, but depending on the performance of your computer, this may not be the best approach. To learn more about managing your system's performance, see Appendix B, "Performance and Rendering."

Using the Pan and Scan Effect

The Pan and Scan effect is another type of effect that is usually applied to a filler track rather than an individual clip. These effects are used when delivering alternate aspect ratio versions of a program. For example, you may be editing a program shot in 16:9 but be required to deliver a 4:3 version.

Since the program we are working in is formatted as 16:9, let's generate a 4:3 version. This is typically done by creating a duplicate version of the sequence with the Reformat effect applied.

To make at 4:3 version of a 16:9 sequence:

1. Choose **WINDOWS > 1 RTS PT2 FX SEQUENCES**.

2. In the RTS PT2 FX Sequences bin window, double-click the **RTS FX PT2 LESSON 07B** sequence. The sequence appears in the Record monitor. This is our duplicate sequence.

3. Press **CTRL+8** (Windows) or **COMMAND+8** (Mac) to open the Effect Palette.

4. Choose the **REFORMAT** effects category then drag the **PAN AND SCAN** effect to V3 in the Timeline. Your sequence should look like that in Figure 7.27.

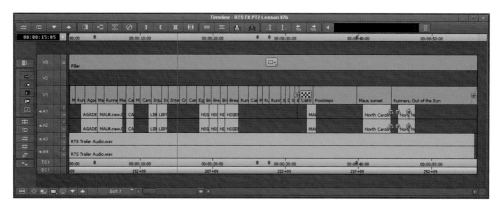

Figure 7.27
Pan and Scan effect applied to V3.

5. Enter Effect mode and click on the newly applied clip to see its parameters in the Effect Editor. (See Figure 7.28.)

    The Aspect Ratios parameter group is the key set of parameters for this effect. You use them to tell the system the sequence's current aspect ratio and choose the desired output aspect ratio.

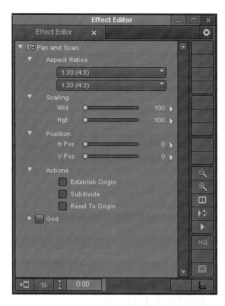

Figure 7.28
Pan and Scan effect parameters.

6. Choose **16:9 ANAMORPHIC** from the upper pop-up menu. The other 16:9 option, 1.78 (16:9), is to be used only for 16:9 letterboxed material, not full-screen 16:9.

7. A box appears in the Effect preview in the Record monitor, showing you the 16:9 region that will be extracted. (See Figure 7.29.) By default, the center of the 16:9 frame is extracted to 4:3.

Figure 7.29
4:3 extraction region.

8. Exit Effect mode. The extracted region is resized to take up the full frame. To see the final 4:3 version correctly, you should change the Composer window's aspect ratio.

Tip: Sometimes a simple center extraction is not appropriate for every shot in the sequence. The Pan and Scan effect includes an enable button, Subdivide Effect, that allows you to automatically break the Pan and Scan effect up into multiple effects—one for every edit on a given track. Simply enable the video track you wish to base your subdivision on and then select the Subdivide enable button. You can then make adjustments to the position of the extraction for every clip in your edit.

9. Right-click on the Composer window and choose **PROJECT ASPECT RATIO > 4:3**. (See Figure 7.30.) The Composer window switches to 4:3, and the extraction is properly displayed.

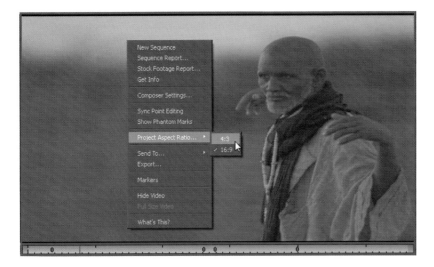

Figure 7.30
Project Aspect
Ratio options.

10. Toggle the video monitor between V3 and V2 to switch between the original 16:9 version and the reformatted 4:3 version. You can use a single sequence for both outputs as long as you remember to set the video monitor to the proper track. That said, it is recommended that you make a duplicate sequence version and properly name it so you do not output the wrong version.

11. In the RTS PT2 FX Sequences bin window, click the **RTS FX PT2 LESSON 07B** sequence's name and append **4x3 VERSION** to the end.

Review/Discussion Questions

1. How is a Picture-in-Picture effect different from other effects we've worked with so far, such as the Resize effect?

2. Why should you crop blanking out of the frame?

3. How else can cropping be used?

4. Why are keyframes required at the beginning and end of an animation?

5. What does the Reverse Animation parameter do?

6. What keys must you hold down on the keyboard to make sure that a segment move only moves a clip vertically and does not shift its position in time?

7. If you add a keyframe via the Record monitor, what parameters are keyframed?

8. Why might you want to use the Remove Redundant Keyframes command?

9. What happens to the animation if you switch keyframes from linear to spline interpolation?

10. How do nests of effects like PIP differ from those of other effects?

11. What can you change within a title nest?

12. When should you nest rather than layer?

13. When should you layer rather than nest?

14. What is the Pan and Scan effect used for?

Lesson 7 Keyboard Shortcuts

Key	Shortcut
Ctrl+Y (Windows)/Command+Y (Mac)	New video track
Ctrl+8 (Windows)/Command+8 (Mac)	Open Effect Editor

Creating Banners and Split Screens

Let's return to *Hell's Kitchen* and use multilayer effects to add a bit of drama to the sequence opening. You will be creating a split screen and using a PIP to create a background for a title.

Media Used:

Hell's Kitchen

Duration:

20 minutes

GOALS

- Crop to create a horizontal banner to run under the clock time title

- Use PIPs to create a split screen of a member from the blue and red team

Use the Exercise 07 sequence in the Hells Kitchen PT2 project, found in the HK Exercises bin. Here are the producer's notes for each of the shots:

- **Clock title.** I'd like a banner to be placed behind the title. It should be made of blurry fire and extend from the left edge of the frame to enclose the text. There should be a small and equal amount of margin above, below, and to the right of the text. You can find a clip of fire in the HK Video Source Clips bin.

- **Split screen.** As the voiceover switches from the blue team to the red team, I'd like a split screen of a member of the blue team and Elise from the red team to animate in to help emphasize the different performance of the two teams. I'd like the two shots to split the screen evenly horizontally and be slightly offset vertically. The split should enter and exit to match the sfx in the audio.

To accomplish these effects, you will need to use the following skills you learned during this lesson:

- Use cropping to create the fire banner and to make sure the split screens focus on the characters rather than the background.

- Use Add Edit, Match Frame, and Trim to isolate the effect's timing of the split and overlay the second clip.

- Use keyframes to create the split-in and split-out animation. The markers will help you set the timing.

Keying and Mattes

Let's say you're making a film and you need a shot of someone on the moon, or you need a shot of your star actor hanging from a burning building. You can get those shots if you know how to create composites and, to start with, how to key.

Media Used: Agent Zero

Duration: 60 minutes

GOALS

- Learn the different types of keys
- Apply SpectraMatte
- Explore the SpectraMatte Analysis Display
- Create a garbage mask
- Refine the matte channel

Different Keying Types

Keying means to create transparency in a foreground image and combine it with a background image to create one composite image. To create a composite, you select a portion of the foreground that will be transparent. The transparent portion is called the *matte channel*. One of the most common ways to create a matte channel is to use a keyer effect.

A *keyer* is a procedural effect, which means it generates a matte based on an algorithm and not a shape or mask that you create. Keyers can create transparency based on the luminance or chrominance in an image. Either way, successful keying depends on planning.

The foreground should be shot in a manner that helps generate the matte. The most common way is to isolate it against an evenly lit, solid-color background, typically a blue or green screen. Special types of keyers have been developed to generate a matte from a blue or green background, commonly referred to as a *chroma key*. A more precise term would be *color difference key*. A chroma key is a simple effect that picks a color range and generates a matte from only those pixels. Today, more effective blue and green screen keyers typically employ an analysis method called *color difference keying*. The simple explanation is that there's more math involved in color difference keying to separate blue or green from the foreground image. It basically subtracts (or gets the difference from) the selected color and the other color channels. When used on primary colors (red, green, or blue), the result is a better matte. Because there are a lot of red hues in nature, especially skin tones, keying is usually done against a green or blue screen.

Note: The terms *mask* and *matte* are often used interchangeably. In this book, *mask* refers to a shape that is used to limit an effect to certain areas. *Matte* refers to a grayscale image used to identify transparency in an RGB image.

Applying SpectraMatte

Media Composer includes a number of different keyers, but the best keyer for blue or green screen is the SpectraMatte effect. SpectraMatte not only provides a better quality key compared to the RGB keyer effect, it also makes it easy to fine-tune your keys and to solve problems such as controlling shadows and removing color spill. In this lesson, you'll work with a simple sequence that includes two layers all set up for some green screen keying.

To use SpectraMatte:

1. Open Media Composer, select **AGENT ZERO PT2** in the Projects list, and click **OK**. The Project window opens and lists two bins.

2. Double-click the **AZ PT2 FX SEQUENCES** bin in the Project window.

3. In the bin that opens, double-click the **AZ PT2 KEYING-START** sequence with the man on the green screen (see Figure 8.1). The sequence appears in the Record monitor. This is a scene from an independent film, *Agent Zero*, which is a takeoff on the spy genre.

Figure 8.1
Load the AZ PT2 Keying-START sequence of the man on the green screen into the Record monitor.

4. To get an understanding of the content, click the **VIDEO TRACK MONITOR** button for track V1. This displays the background that your subject will be composited on (see Figure 8.2).

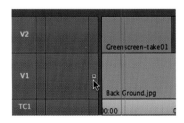

Figure 8.2
Click the V1 Video Track Monitor button to display the background.

5. Click the V2 **VIDEO TRACK MONITOR** button to view the green screen foreground. Your task is to make the green screen transparent from the foreground image to reveal the V1 background track under it. When setting up the tracks for a green or blue screen composite, the foreground subject should always be placed on a track directly above the background segment.

6. Press the **SPACE BAR** to play the sequence to see the movement in the clip.

7. When you are finished watching the sequence, apply the SpectraMatte effect to the foreground image on V2. The effect is available in the Key category of the Effect Palette. Choose **TOOLS > EFFECT PALETTE** or press **COMMAND+8** (Mac) or **CTRL+8** (Windows) to open the Effect Palette window.

8. Select the **KEY** category and drag the **SPECTRAMATTE** effect onto the green screen segment on V2; then click the **EFFECT MODE** button to enter Effect mode. When you enter Effect mode, the Source Monitor shows the SpectraGraph screen (see Figure 8.3). The dark wedge on the screen provides visual feedback on the color that is being keyed.

Figure 8.3
The SpectraGraph screen provides visual feedback on the color range being keyed.

9. As you can see in the figure, the wedge is nowhere near green, and consequently our image in the Effect Preview monitor still shows the green screen background. To select green as the key color, position the pointer over the Color Preview window to activate the eyedropper (see Figure 8.4).

Figure 8.4
Click the Color Preview window to activate the eyedropper.

10. Press and hold the mouse button, drag the eyedropper to the Effect Preview monitor, and release the mouse button over the green screen, close to the subject (see Figure 8.5).

Figure 8.5
Drag the eyedropper anywhere over the green screen, then release the mouse button.

Media Composer updates the Red, Green, and Blue parameter numeric values in the Effect Editor, and the SpectraGraph screen now has the wedge placed over the green, indicating that is the color being used to generate the matte. Most importantly, the Effect Preview monitor now shows a very nice composite of the foreground and background.

Understanding the SpectraGraph Screen

The SpectraGraph screen shows a color wheel–style swatch that represents the color space within which the SpectraMatte effect works. The center point of the swatch is neutral gray. As you move around the swatch, the hue changes, and as you move away from the center, the saturation increases. The darkened wedge in the SpectraGraph screen shows the range of color used to generate the matte. The wedge gets wider at the perimeter of the color swatch, keying out a relatively broad range of highly saturated colors from the chosen key color.

Since green screens and blue screens should be well lit, highly saturated colors—and those colors rarely exist in nature—at the perimeter of the swatch are the kinds of color values that should always require keying out. That's in a perfect world; many times you have poorly lit green/blue screens, so the wedge also provides very precise control over low-saturation color values and hue color values. These colors fall on the borderline between those you want to key out and those you want to retain. These are the kinds of color values that you often need to blend or fine-tune—for example, to improve the edges of the foreground subject in a key shot.

The SpectraMatte effect calculates the key color wedge from some of the main parameter values you set. Picking the key color sets the position of the wedge around the color swatch. The Chroma Control Tolerance parameter defines the width or spread of the wedge. The saturation value set by the Chroma Control Key Saturation parameter defines the location of the center point of the wedge. You can move the wedge out from the center of the swatch by increasing the Key Saturation value. Many of the other parameters modify how this basic key color wedge is calculated.

Superimposed on the color swatch is a vectorscope-style display that shows the distribution of color values in the foreground image. This typically shows a concentration of either green or blue color values that represent the background screen color you want to key out, along with the distribution of other color values from the foreground subject that you want to retain.

The SpectraGraph screen lets you clearly see the relationship between the current result of the key and the color values in your image. Knowing this, you can make further parameter adjustments that remove these values more completely from the key. By viewing both the SpectraGraph screen and the standard view of the composited images, you get all the information you need to produce a high-quality key.

Creating a Garbage Mask

In this particular green screen setup and many others, large portions of the shot are just green screen, and the subject never crosses over them. In these cases you can simplify the keying task by using a *garbage mask* to remove unwanted portions from the outer areas of the frame. A garbage mask allows you to focus on removing the green screen that is immediately around the subject rather than having to key out the entire green screen. You create a garbage mask by drawing complex spline shapes or simply cropping the image as tightly as possible without cutting off any of the subject. Whatever method you use, it's a good idea to create the garbage mask early in the keying process so that you don't waste time perfecting an area that is easily masked out.

To create a garbage mask:

1. SpectraMatte includes cropping controls for creating simple garbage masks. In the Effect Editor, click the **CROP** disclosure triangle to reveal the parameters for the top, bottom, left, and right sides of the frame (see Figure 8.6).

Figure 8.6
Click the disclosure triangle to reveal the Crop parameters.

2. We only want to crop the right and left sides because cropping the top or bottom of the frame would cut off portions of our subject. Under the Effect Preview monitor, drag the position bar to roughly **01:00:00:15**. This is the point in the clip where the subject is as far to the left as he gets (see Figure 8.7). We'll use this frame as the guide for our left-side crop.

Figure 8.7
Drag the position bar to roughly 01:00:00:15.

3. Drag the **L** slider representing the left-side crop until it displays around **340**. You can see that the tip of the gun is cropped off. The 340 setting is too far, so you'll need to decrease the crop amount. Drag the **L** slider back to around **300**. Here the gun is not cropped, so we can leave it at this setting.

4. Under the Effect Preview monitor, drag the position bar to the end of the effect. This is the point in the clip where the subject is as far to the right as he gets (see Figure 8.8). We'll use this frame as the guide for our right side crop.

Figure 8.8
Drag the position bar to the end of the effect.

5. Drag the **R** slider representing the right side crop until it displays around **-115**. You can see the man's back is cropped off. The −115 setting is too far, so you'll need to decrease the crop amount. Drag the **R** slider back to around **-90**. Here his back is not cropped, so we can leave it at this setting.

6. Under the Effect Preview monitor, click the **PLAY IN TO OUT** button to view the crop and ensure that none of the subject is cropped during the clip. You may have to play the clip a few times to be certain.

With your garbage mask in place, you can now refine the matte you created in the first section.

Refining the Matte Channel

As good as this composite looks, there are flaws. The SpectraMatte effect includes a number of ways to improve the key and make it more believable. You'll be able to see the imperfections more clearly if you view the matte, so that's our first step.

To refine the matte channel:

1. In the **MATTE ANALYSIS** section of the Effect Editor, choose **ALPHA IN SOURCE MONITOR** from the **SPECTRAGRAPH SOURCE MONITOR** menu (see Figure 8.9). The grayscale matte channel is now displayed in the Source monitor with the crop settings revealing the background clip.

Figure 8.9
Choose Alpha in Source Monitor to display the matte channel in the Source Monitor.

2. The white areas of the matte represent the opaque parts of the foreground image. The black areas represent the transparent parts. The first step in refining your matte is to create solid white and solid black. By refining the key color using the Chroma controls, you can achieve a more solid-looking matte. Drag both the **KEY SAT LINE** and the **KEY SATURATION** sliders to **20** until the matte is solid back and white (see Figure 8.10). Raising these two parameters keys out a wider range of low-saturation color values from the foreground image.

Figure 8.10
Drag both Key Sat Line and Key Saturation to 20 until the matte is solid black and white.

3. To remove any lingering specks of white from the black background, adjust the **INNER SOFTNESS** slider to **35**. Inner Softness determines how harsh a cutoff or smooth a blend is used between the keyed-out color and the foreground. The higher the number, the more color values on the border of the wedge in SpectraGraph are completely keyed out rather than blended.

4. With a good solid black and white matte channel, it's time to focus on the edges of the foreground. This is often the most difficult area of a matte, so it gets special attention in the Matte Processing section of the Effects Editor. The Matte Processing controls let you blur, erode, or dilate the edges of the matte channel to make the matte fit better around your subject. In this case, we'll erode the matte a small amount to remove any dark matte lines or haloing effect that may exist. Click the disclosure triangle for **MATTE PROCESSING** to reveal the Matte Processing menu.

5. Choose **ERODE** from the **MATTE PROCESSING** menu, then drag the **MATTE BLUR** slider to **5**. (See the results in Figure 8.11.)

Figure 8.11
The matte channel after applying Erode.

6. Lastly, we'll correct for any green "spill" that has reflected off the green screen and fallen on the foreground subject. Spill suppression lets you remove any reflected key color that is on the foreground and replaces it with magenta. When working with subtle changes like spill suppression, it is sometimes easier to zoom in to the image to see more detail. From the right side of the Effect Editor, click the **ENLARGE** button twice. The image in the Effect Preview monitor is enlarged.

7. Holding down the **COMMAND+OPTION** keys (Mac) or the **ALT+CTRL** keys (Windows), click and drag in the Effect Preview monitor to pan the image until you see the subject's hands and forearms centered on screen (see Figure 8.12). This is where you'll see the most difference from spill suppression.

Figure 8.12
Enlarge and pan the Effect Preview monitor so subtle spill changes are easier to see.

8. There are two parameters for spill suppression. You can change the spread of the spill correction using the Spill Angle Offset parameter. Larger adjustments usually result in too much color correction of the foreground image, but subtle adjustments can neutralize the green spill without adding too much magenta. Drag the SPILL ANGLE OFFSET parameter to **50**.

9. Saturation determines the threshold for where spill suppression begins. The higher the number, the more key color with less saturation will be included in the suppression (see Figure 8.13). Drag the SPILL SATURATION slider to **50**.

Figure 8.13
Detailed view after spill suppression is applied.

10. To return the enlarged image to its original size in the Effect Preview monitor, click twice on the **REDUCE** button on the right side of the Effect Editor.

11. Under the Effect Preview monitor, click the **PLAY IN TO OUT** button to view the composite. Play the composite a few times to bask in the glow of a job well done.

These basic steps can be used to produce high-quality composites on almost any green or blue screen. There are times when mattes may need more work, and your garbage mask may need a more refined shape. You can learn how to handle more complicated keying scenarios in the book *Media Composer 6: Advanced Effects and Compositing.*

Review/Discussion Questions

1. The transparent channel in a clip is called

   a. The green screen

   b. Luminance

   c. A matte

2. True or false: The SpectraMatte effect provides a better key than the RGB keyer effect, and it also makes it easier to fine-tune your keys.

3. If you have a background clip on track V2, what track should your green screen clip be edited onto?

4. What do the L and R parameters stand for in the Crop Parameter group of the SpectraMatte?

5. True or false: The purpose of a garbage mask is to remove all of the green or blue screen from the foreground.

6. What is the Alpha in Source Monitor menu selection used for?

Lesson 8 Keyboard Shortcut

Key	Shortcut
Ctrl+8 (Windows)/Command+8 (Mac)	**Open Effect Palette**

Keying on Different Backgrounds

On the same sequence and background you have been using, use the two additional clips found in the Greenscreen Clips bin to create two additional composites.

Media Used:

Agent Zero

Duration:

15 minutes

GOALS

- Create two additional composites using the SpectraMatte effect

1. In the Project window, double-click the **GREENSCREEN CLIPS** bin to open it.

2. Make two titles in the Title tool. On the first, create a bright orange rectangle that fills the screen.

3. Save the title in the Greenscreen Clips bin and call it **ORANGE 02**.

4. On the second title, create a crimson rectangle that fills the screen.

5. Save the title to the Greenscreen Clips bin and call it **CRIMSON 03**.

6. On V1, edit in six seconds of the **ORANGE 02** title right after the first Key effect is completed in the sequence.

7. Edit in four seconds of the **CRIMSON 03** title on V1 right after the **ORANGE 02** title.

8. Edit the unused **GREENSCREEN TAKE 02** clip on V2 over the orange background.

9. Edit the unused **GREENSCREEN TAKE 03** clip on V2 over the crimson background.

10. Apply a **COLOR EFFECT** to boost the saturation on the green-screen clips.

11. Add a **SPECTRAMATTE** effect to both clips, keeping the Color Effect as well.

12. Use the **SCALING** and **CROPPING** parameters in SpectraMatte to crop out some of the unwanted garbage in the green-screen clip.

13. Adjust the **TOLERANCE**, **KEY SAT LINE**, **KEY SAT**, and **SOFTNESS** settings on both clips to get the best result.

14. Adjust the **SPILL** settings on both clips to remove any green spill.

3D Title Animation with Marquee

As you move toward completion of your sequence, you might need to display titles over the video or add text slates or other graphical elements in this finishing stage. The Avid Marquee Title tool enables you to create and add these elements easily.

Media Used: Agent Zero

Duration: 60 minutes

GOALS

- Create text in Marquee
- Format and layer
- Modify colors, materials, and surfaces
- Rotate and extrude text
- Save text styles
- Animate objects in a scene
- Save titles to a bin
- Generate AutoTitles

Creating Text in Marquee

The Avid Marquee Title tool creates pages of text and graphics that can be saved over a color background or keyed over video. Many of the formatting options in Marquee will seem familiar to you because they are similar to those found in the Avid Title tool as well as almost every word processor.

To create text using the Avid Marquee Title tool:

1. Open Media Composer, select the **AGENT ZERO PT 2** project from the list of projects, and then click **OK**.

2. In the Project window, double-click the **AZ PT2 SEQUENCES** bin to open it and double-click the **AZ PT2 MARQUEE-START** sequence in the bin to load it into the Record monitor.

3. Play the sequence until you see the man on the roof between the IN and OUT marks, as shown in Figure 9.1. This is where we want the title to appear. The frame you stop on will be visible as a reference background when making the title in Marquee.

Figure 9.1
Play the sequence until you see the man on the roof.

Tip: While you are in Marquee, Media Composer will not auto-save your project or bins. Before opening Marquee, manually save any bins you have changed since the last auto-save.

4. You can create titles using either the standard Avid Title tool or the Marquee 3D Title tool. For this book we'll cover the standard Marquee 3D Title tool. You can learn more about the Avid Title tool in the book *Media Composer 6: Part I–Editing Essentials*. To begin, select **CLIP > NEW TITLE**.

5. A dialog box appears allowing you to choose between the Avid Title tool and Marquee. Since we want to create 3D animated titles for this lesson, select **PERSIST** and then click **MARQUEE** to open the Marquee Title Tool window. For the rest of this editing session, Media Composer will automatically open Marquee and bypass this dialog box.

6. The Marquee Title tool opens with the video frame from the sequence as a reference, as shown in Figure 9.2. (If there is no sequence in the Timeline, the Marquee tool opens with a black background.) The default Marquee window includes all the tools you need for basic title creation. The Monitor window is where you create your text and graphics. As with Media Composer, you can select or create toolsets to display the tools and window layout you want. Select **TOOLSET > BASIC** or press **F2** to configure the window layout in its basic mode.

Figure 9.2
Marquee opens with the frame currently displayed in the sequence as a reference.

Note: When the Marquee tool opens, the dimensions and frame rate are always based on the current project.

7. You place text in a scene using the Text tool. Select the **TEXT** tool (or press **T**), as shown in Figure 9.3. The cursor becomes an arrow with an I-beam. Click anywhere in the frame to add text. A red bounding box and an insertion point appear where you click.

Figure 9.3
Select the Text tool (or press T) and click in the frame to begin typing.

8. Type the word **AGENT**. The bounding box expands as you type.

9. When you finish typing, click the **EDIT** tool as shown in Figure 9.4 to return the pointer to an arrow. When you return to the Edit tool, handles appear around the bounding box.

Figure 9.4
Click the Edit tool when you have finished typing.

10. To type a different line of text, select the **TEXT** tool (or press **T**) and press **0** (zero). As long as you do not type directly over the word AGENT, Marquee will create a new text object. Click the **EDIT** tool when you are done.

11. You can display outlines around the frame to use as guidelines for safe title and safe action areas, as shown in Figure 9.5. Select **VIEW > SAFE ACTION/TITLE**.

Figure 9.5
Select View > Safe Action/Title to display guidelines for safe layout areas.

The safe title area is the inner box. All text for television broadcast should remain within this inner box. The safe action area is the outer box. This is the area for video display. Now you can begin formatting text to fit within the safe title guides.

Formatting and Layering Text

When you work in Marquee, the Edit tool is used to select an object; when an object is selected, you can perform operations on it. In this section, you'll perform some fundamental operations such as changing the font, font size, text position, and layering order.

To change the formatting and layer order of text:

1. You use the Text Formatting section of the toolbar to adjust font, font size, text style, text justification, and kerning and leading. To change the font, select the **AGENT** text and select **TREBUCHET MS** from the **FONT** menu at the top of the window.

2. With the AGENT text selected, drag the value shuttle up to **150** to increase the font size, as shown in Figure 9.6.

Figure 9.6
Drag the value shuttle up to 150 to increase the font size.

3. Although you can create text at a specific font size, you can also make it larger or smaller by scaling it. With the Edit tool, select the number **O** and then place the cursor near one of the bounding-box handles.

4. When the cursor becomes an up arrow, press Shift+Alt-drag (Windows) or Shift+Option-drag (Mac) the handle until the 0 is touching the safe action guidelines at the top and bottom of the frame, as shown in Figure 9.7. Holding the modifier keys as you drag retains the aspect ratio of the text. You may have to change the handle you drag on as your text grows.

Figure 9.7
With the cursor near a handle, hold down modifier keys while you drag to change the text size.

Tip: To retain the text's aspect ratio and scale from the center point, press
      Shift+Ctrl+Alt (Windows) or Shift+Command+Option (Mac) as you drag
      the handle.

5. Using the Edit tool, you can reposition title objects by dragging them in
    the Monitor window. Click and drag inside the 0 text box (but not the
    handles) to center it over the man in the video frame.

Tip: To nudge the position of text using the keyboard, press an arrow key.

6. You can change how objects appear in front of or behind other objects.
    Make sure the number 0 is still selected and select OBJECT > SEND
    BACKWARD. The number 0 is now placed behind the AGENT text,
    making it easier to select the AGENT text.

7. To center the AGENT text, we'll use a convenient alignment grid that
    the text can snap to. Select VIEW > GRID to display the alignment grid
    in the Marquee window.

8. The grid is made up of a series of dots that objects can snap to while
    dragging. Click and drag the **AGENT** text until it is roughly in the center
    of the Marquee window, as shown in Figure 9.8.

Figure 9.8
After displaying the grid, position the AGENT text until it is centered in the frame.

9. To turn off the grind, select VIEW > GRID.

With the text now laid out, formatted, and sized, it's time to turn our attention
toward the look of the text. A combination of colors, materials, and surface attrib-
utes can give text a unique look.

Modifying Colors, Materials, and Surfaces

You can select the color for text, shadows, and other objects. You can select a color from a Color menu, use an eyedropper to select a color from any open application on your computer, or use the Marquee Color Picker.

To add gradient color blends, drop shadows, and edges to text:

1. Objects in Marquee can have several surfaces, which can all have different colors. The main surface covers the whole object, making it easy to create simple, single-colored text or shapes. To apply a single color to the AGENT text, select it with the Edit tool and then make sure that **ENABLE MAIN SURFACE** is selected in the **MAIN SURFACE** area of the Quick Titles Properties window.

2. Click the button next to the **BASE** color well in the Quick Titles Properties window. The Color menu appears, as shown in Figure 9.9.

Figure 9.9
Click the button next to the Base color well to view the Color menu.

3. Pick a vibrant red color from the color swatches in the top area of the Color menu.

4. You can also create a blend between two colors using the gradient controls. With the **AGENT** text still selected, click the **ENABLE GRADIENT** check box. The gradient controls become available, and a gradient is applied to the text.

5. By default, the gradient moves from black on the left to the color in the color well on the right (red, in this case). To change the starting color of the gradient, right-click the triangular color stop on the left side of the gradient bar to display the **COLOR** menu as shown in Figure 9.10 and select a bright yellow color. Because the Tint control is enabled, the gradient turns completely red.

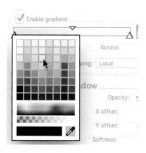

Figure 9.10
To create a gradient, right-click the color stop to display the Color menu.

Note: When you define a gradient, it is important to understand the concept of tinting in Marquee. You can use the base color for a surface to tint a gradient. The result is a new color that combines the base color and the gradient colors. If you are defining a gradient, and the final colors on your title object's surface are not what you expect, you might need to deselect Tint.

6. Deselect the **TINT** check box. Now you can set the ending color value in the gradient.

7. Right-click the far-right color stop to display the **COLOR** menu and select a bright red color. The gradient is applied locally, meaning each letter has a gradient going from yellow to red across it (see Figure 9.11).

Figure 9.11
The gradient is applied locally across each letter.

Note: To adjust the opacity, click in the Opacity ramp of the Color menu or the A (Alpha) slider in the Color dialog box. The left end represents full transparency; the right end represents full opacity.

8. To control how the gradient is mapped to the object's surface, you can use the Mapping menu. Select **CONTAINER** in the **MAPPING** menu so the gradient is applied across the bounding box container. (See Figure 9.12.)

Figure 9.12
Select Container so the gradient is applied across the bounding box container.

9. To change the direction of the gradient so it covers the letters top to bottom instead of left to right, click the center **GRADIENT TYPE** button as shown in Figure 9.13. The red begins at the bottom, and the yellow is at the top of the text.

Figure 9.13
Click the center Gradient Type button
to change the gradient direction.

10. To reverse the direction, click the center **GRADIENT TYPE** button again. The gradient switches direction, but it appears to be mostly yellow. Although the gradient appears to be applied to the text, it is actually sized to the bounding box. Depending on the size and placement of the bounding box with respect to the text, the gradient mapping results will vary.

11. To map the gradient so equal amounts of red and yellow are spread across the text, hover the pointer over the lower-right corner bounding box handle until the point changes to an up arrow.

12. Drag the lower-right corner down until it is just past the lower-right corner of the letter T, as shown in Figure 9.14. As you drag, you'll notice the gradient spreading more evenly across the letters.

Figure 9.14
Drag the lower-right corner down until it is just past the lower-right corner of the letter T.

13. Adding a drop shadow to a title gives the perception of depth, as though the title were lying on a different plane than the video beneath. With the **AGENT** text still selected, enable the **SHOW DROP SHADOW** check box in the Quick Title window. The drop shadow is added, and the Drop Shadow controls are highlighted in the Quick Title window.

14. To adjust the shadow's position, click the **Shadow** tool and drag the cursor around until the shadow box is to the lower left, as shown in Figure 9.15. The black L-shape represents the location of the shadow relative to the object. Release the mouse, and the shadow on the text updates.

Figure 9.15

To position the shadow, click the Shadow tool and drag the cursor around.

15. Adjust the shadow's softness by typing a value of **25** in the **Softness** text box.

16. Finally, we'll add a border around the edge of the text. Enable the **Change Edge Properties** check box in the Quick Titles window.

17. You can choose different styles of edging from the pop-up menu, as shown in Figure 9.16. Select **Flat Border** from the **Edge Type** pop-up menu.

Figure 9.16

Choose different styles of edging from the pop-up menu.

18. To select the color of the edge, click the button next to the color well. The Color menu appears. Select a black color for the edge. A thin black edge is displayed around the text.

The Quick Titles window handles most of the fundamental text-formatting properties that you'll use on a day-to-day basis. There are many other text options in Marquee that can really set your titles apart. You'll use two of those options in the next lesson.

Rotating and Extruding Text

Up to this point, you haven't really done anything that you couldn't do in the Avid Title tool. That changes now. One of Marquee's stand-out capabilities is 3D rotation and extrusion. Let's start by creating a 3D metallic look for the number 0. There are a few pieces to creating this look: You need to add a texture, some lights, a bevel, and extrusion.

To add an extruded 3D metallic look to text:

1. Select the number **0** in the Marquee window.

2. Instead of using a simple color or gradient, you'll apply a texture to the number. Marquee includes a number of useful textures, but you can also create your own. In the Styles Library, click the **Textures** tab. If the Library window isn't open, select **Window > Library > Textures.**

3. Click the **Avid Textures +** sign (Windows) or disclosure triangle (Mac) to reveal the included textures, as shown in Figure 9.17. Double-click a few of the textures to try them out. When you double-click a texture, it is applied to the selected object.

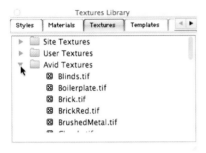

Figure 9.17
In the Textures tab, click the Avid Textures + sign (Windows) or disclosure triangle (Mac) to reveal the included textures.

4. Scroll down to the **Metal.tif** texture and double-click it to apply it to the number 0.

5. You can use the Surfaces Properties tab to modify the texture. A quick way to open the Surfaces Properties tab is to right-click (Windows) or Control-click (Mac) on the **Transform** tab and select **Properties > Surfaces** from the pop-up menu. You can also select **Window > Properties > Surfaces.**

6. In the Surfaces Properties window, click the **Enable Lighting** check box (see Figure 9.18) and lower the **Shininess** parameter to **4.0**. Enabling lighting makes 3D text more realistic (see Figure 9.19). Lowering the Shininess parameter spreads the specular highlight more, making the lighting more even.

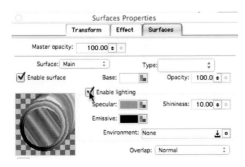

Figure 9.18
Click the Enable Lighting check box.

Figure 9.19
Lighting makes 3D text more realistic.

7. Click the **EFFECT** tab (or select **WINDOW > PROPERTIES > EFFECT**). The Effect tab in the Properties window controls the 3D bevel styles as well as the extrusion amount.

8. From the **EDGE TYPE** pop-up menu, select **EMBOSS**. This adds a slight rim around the number, giving it a bit more depth.

9. To add thickness to the number, drag the **EXTRUDE DEPTH** parameter to **15**.

10. Although there is a change to the look of the number, it's difficult to see the real impact extrusion has on it because the number is still facing straight on to the screen. You can add a slight rotation to make the extrusion more obvious. To rotate objects in Marquee, you use the Rotate tool. Click the **ROTATE** tool in the toolbox as shown in Figure 9.20.

Figure 9.20
Click the Rotate tool in the toolbox.

11. When you select the Rotate tool, a rotation sphere appears around the selected object. The rotation sphere consists of three color-coded rotation circles and three matching axes with crosshairs at either end. To tilt the object forward and backward, drag the yellow X rotation circle. To rotate the object like a clock, drag the green Z rotation circle. In this case we would like to spin or pivot the number so it faces slightly off center to the left. Place the pointer directly over the blue **Y** rotation ring until your cursor changes to a crosshair.

12. Drag the blue ring slightly to the left to rotate the number as shown in Figure 9.21.

Figure 9.21
Drag the blue ring slightly to the left to rotate the number.

You now have a true 3D object with a metallic texture and shine to it.

Saving Text Styles

If you like the look of an object that you have created, you can save the look as a style to use again later.

To save text styles for reuse:

1. Select the number **O** if it's not still selected, then click the **STYLES** tab in the Texture Library window. If the Texture Library window is not already open, select **WINDOW > LIBRARY > STYLES**.

2. Right-click (Windows) or Control-click (Mac) the **USER STYLES** folder to place the new style there, and select **NEW STYLES** as shown in Figure 9.22.

Figure 9.22
Right-click (Windows) or Control-click (Mac) the User Styles folder to place the new style there, and select New Styles.

Note: You cannot place a new style into the Avid Styles folder. If you right-click (Windows) or Control-click (Mac) an individual style definition, the new style will be placed in the same folder as the selected definition.

3. You can modify the set of properties that will be saved in the new style. In particular, you probably do not want to save the position and size of the object. Deselect the **CONTAINER** and **TRANSFORM** properties so these properties are not included in your style.

4. Type **LOW SHINE 3D METALLIC** for the new style in the **NAME** text box and then click **OK**.

The new style appears in the User Styles folder in the Styles Library window. When you are ready to reuse the style, just select the object in the Marquee window and double-click your saved style.

Animating Objects in a Scene

Now that the text is formatted, aligned, textured, and saved, it's time to focus on the other parts of the title. Next we'll look at how the Marquee animation mode works and we'll adjust the timing in the Timeline.

To create movement on text:

1. The easiest way to show the basic animation tools is to select a toolset. Select TOOLSET > BASIC ANIMATION. The Basic Animation toolset adds the Animation Mode button at the top of the toolbox and places the Timeline at the bottom of the Marquee window, as shown in Figure 9.23.

Figure 9.23
The Basic Animation toolset adds the Animation Mode button at the top of the toolbox and places the Timeline at the bottom of the Marquee window.

2. Click the **Animation Mode** button at the top of the toolbar to enable it. (See Figure 9.24.) When the Animation Mode button is enabled, any change you make to an object either on screen or by changing a property value will create a keyframe.

Figure 9.24
Click the Animation Mode button to enable it.

3. Make sure the blue position indicator is at the start of the Timeline. (You may need to scroll the Timeline window to be sure you at the beginning.) Then drag the **AGENT** text to the left side of the screen. (See Figure 9.25.)

Figure 9.25
Drag the AGENT text on the left side of screen.

4. Click the timecode bar to move the blue position indicator to the middle of the Timeline, as shown in Figure 9.26.

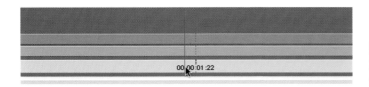

Figure 9.26
Move the position indicator
to the center of the Timeline.

5. Drag the **AGENT** text back to its original position in the center of the screen. You've now created an animation.

6. To play the animation, go back to the start of the Timeline and press the **SPACE BAR** or click the **PLAY** button at the bottom of the Timeline.

7. Choose EDIT > UNDO TRANSLATE OBJECT; then choose it again to undo the animation completely.

8. Click the ANIMATION MODE button to disable it. (Leaving it on could lead to animations you never intended to create.)

As you've just seen, the Marquee Timeline works similarly to Media Composer. Just like Media Composer, the Marquee Timeline enables you to move to specific points in time and shows you the relationships among objects in a scene. A scene is constructed of layers that contain stacked tracks representing the objects. Layers and objects on higher tracks appear in front of layers and objects on lower tracks. You can see and modify where various objects start and end in time, as well as how object properties change value over time. Next we'll trim a clip, add a fade up, and add an animation with keyframes. First, however, you must expand the layer container that the objects are within.

To trim a clip, add a fade up, and add an animation:

1. Click the EXPAND button on the right side of the L1 track to access the objects as shown in Figure 9.27. Two objects appear above L1: one for the number 0 and the other for the AGENT text.

Figure 9.27
Click the Expand button on the right side of the track to access the objects inside.

2. To ensure you are working on the correct object, click the MUTE button on the left side of the T1 track as shown in Figure 9.28. The number 0 is hidden in the Marquee window. Click the same MUTE button again to unmute the number 0.

Figure 9.28
Click the Mute button on the left side of the T1 track to hide and unhide the object.

3. To change the starting point for the number 0, you trim the T1 track just like you would in Media Composer. Place the pointer over the left end of the **T1** track. The pointer changes to a Trim icon, indicating that you can click and drag to change the starting point of that track.

4. Click and drag the left edge of the **T1** track a little less than halfway through the Timeline, until the track's duration indicates **03:00**, as shown in Figure 9.29.

Figure 9.29
Click and drag the left edge of the track
until the duration indicates 03:00.

5. Click the **PLAY** button at the bottom of the Timeline to view the edited
   track. The AGENT text is onscreen alone, and then roughly halfway
   through, the number 0 pops on behind it.

6. You can easily fade text on and off screen using the Quick Fade button. In
   the Timeline window, move the position indicator a few frames past the
   start of the T1 track by dragging in the Timecode track. Place it roughly
   where you want the number 0 to be at full opacity. Then click the **MARK
   IN** button in the Transport controls or press **I**.

Tip: If you place both the **IN** or **OUT** points outside the object's duration, the object
will not be affected.

7. Click the **QUICK FADE** button in the Timeline as shown in Figure 9.30.
   Without an OUT point, the number 0 gets a fade-up and stays on screen
   until the end of the scene.

Figure 9.30
Click the Quick Fade button in the Timeline.

8. Drag the position indicator to the start of the scene and click the **PLAY**
   button at the bottom of the Timeline. The number 0 now fades into view
   behind the AGENT text. Once you've finished watching the scene, you
   can then focus on animating the AGENT text.

9. Select the **AGENT** text in the Marquee window and then click the
   ANIMATION MODE button in the toolbox, as shown in Figure 9.31.
   To animate the AGENT text, you'll use keyframes to change its rotation
   over time. Any change to a property such as position, rotation, or size
   normally affects that property for the duration of the title. When you
   are in Animation mode, a change that you make to a property affects
   that property only at the current point. When you set different values
   for a property at two different points, Marquee interpolates or fills in the
   values in between for that property, resulting in animation.

Figure 9.31
Click the Animation Mode button in the toolbox.

10. Let's have the AGENT text tilt down at its starting position. Select **WINDOW > PROPERTIES > TRANSFORM** to open the Transform Properties window. Instead of dragging the rotation rings, you can more precisely enter values in the Transform window.

11. Click and drag the **X ROTATION** value shuttle until the value reaches around **80** degrees and the AGENT text is almost completely downward facing but still visible (see Figure 9.32). You've now set the first position in your animation.

Figure 9.32
Drag the X Rotation value shuttle until the AGENT text is facing downward.

Tip: You can reset the rotation in the Transform Properties window by clicking the Reset button for the X, Y, or Z control to the right of the Rotation value shuttle, or right-clicking (Windows) or Control-clicking (Mac) the object in the Marquee window and selecting Reset Rotation from the pop-up menu.

12. In the Timeline, click the **TIMECODE** track at the far left of the Timeline to have the blue position indicator jump to the end of the Timeline. Now you can position the text for the end of the animation.

13. Click and drag the **X ROTATION** value shuttle until the value reaches around **0** and the AGENT text is facing forward (see Figure 9.33).

Figure 9.33
Drag the X Rotation value shuttle until the AGENT text is facing forward.

14. To play your animation, click twice on the **Go to Previous Edit** button at the bottom of the Timeline to place the position indicator at the start of the sequence, and then click **Play**.

15. In addition to animating properties using the property value shuttles, you can also animate an object through the property curves in the Timeline window. These curves show the change in a property's value over time. To begin animating with the property curves, click the **Show Curves** button on the right side of the T1 track as shown in Figure 9.34. The T1 property curve graph appears below the track's title bar.

Figure 9.34
Click the Show Curves button on the right side of the T1 track.

16. To view an existing animation curve, you must enable the Animated property in the Properties list. In the Properties list on the left side of the Timeline window, click the **+** sign (Windows) or disclosure triangle (Mac) for **Transforms** and then again for **Rotation**.

17. The Properties list now shows the X, Y, and Z rotation properties. Click the **X** property as shown in Figure 9.35 to view the rotation animation curve you created previously.

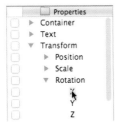

Figure 9.35
Click the + sign (Windows) or disclosure triangle (Mac) for the Transform and Rotation properties.

18. To create new animation, first enable the property you want to change. In the Properties list, click the **+** sign (Windows) or disclosure triangle (Mac) for **Text** and then enable the **Kerning** check box. A red animation curve appears for the Kerning property.

19. You can change the starting point by adjusting the starting keyframe. First, place the position indicator at the start of the Timeline. Hover the mouse over the first keyframe at the start of the kerning animation curve.

20. When the pointer changes to an up arrow, click and drag the keyframe up until the tool tip that is displayed next to the keyframe reaches around **25** as shown in Figure 9.36. Kerning spreads the letters evenly to the right since the text is right-justified by default.

Figure 9.36

When the pointer changes to an up arrow, click and drag the keyframe.

21. Click the center **JUSTIFY** button in the Marquee toolbar at the top of the window to have kerning spread the letters from the center. That sets our first keyframe.

22. To animate, you'll recall that we need at least two keyframes. To add another keyframe for kerning, place the position indicator around the same location that the number 0 comes on screen.

23. Right-click (Windows) or Control-click (Mac) the kerning animation curve and select **INSERT KEY** from the pop-up menu as shown in Figure 9.37.

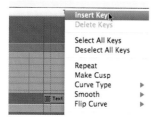

Figure 9.37

Right-click (Windows) or Control-click (Mac) on the kerning animation curve and select Insert Key.

24. Hover the pointer over the newly added keyframe; the pointer changes to an up arrow. Click and drag the keyframe down until the tool tip displayed next to the keyframe reaches around **5**.

25. To play your animation, place the position indicator at the start of the sequence. Then click **PLAY** at the bottom of the Timeline.

You've created your first animation in Marquee. Now it's time to save it to Media Composer.

Saving Titles to a Bin

After you create a new title, you should save and render it. We'll use the Save to Bin option, which renders the title and saves it. If you plan to use your title for television broadcast, you should make sure to activate Safe Colors. This will ensure that only low-saturation colors are used in text, objects, and background.

To save Marquee titles into a Media Composer bin:

1. Select **RENDER > OPTIONS** to open the Render Options window.

2. Select the **USE VIDEO-SAFE COLORS** check box as shown in Figure 9.38 and then click **OK**.

Figure 9.38
Select the Use Video-Safe Colors check box and then click OK.

3. Select **FILE > SAVE TO BIN**. The Save to Avid Bin dialog box appears. Type **AGENT ANIMATION** as the title's name in the **TITLE NAME** text box. Make sure **CURRENT FRAME ONLY (STATIC TITLE)** is not selected and then click **OK** as shown in Figure 9.39. Marquee renders the title.

Figure 9.39
Make sure Current Frame Only (Static Title) is not selected and then click OK to render the title.

4. After the title is rendered, the Save Title dialog box is open unless you have previously saved a title in this session or if you selected Use Same Save Options as Previous Title, If Available. In the Save Title dialog box, select the **AZ PT2 SEQUENCES** bin and a hard drive from the pop-up menus.

5. Select **DNxHD 60 MXF** for the format in the **TITLE FORMATS** area and then click **SAVE**.

Media Composer creates the correct format for the title animation clip and loads it into the Source monitor when finished. It is placed into your target bin. All that's left to do is edit it into your sequence.

Generating AutoTitles

The main title you created earlier is the fun and more creative type of title you get to create for a project. Most of the titles you'll need to create are somewhat more repetitive in nature, such as cast credits. Don't be too concerned about the boredom factor; Marquee has a fast and efficient way you can create a number of titles from a single template. The AutoTitler allows you to create multiple titles, each with different text content, from a single template and an external text file. We'll look at one powerful example: using the AutoTitler to create a few cast and crew credits for a program.

To auto-generate multiple titles from a single template:

1. Using the same Agent Zero project in Media Composer, select CLIP > NEW TITLE to open Marquee.

2. In Marquee, return to a Basic layout by selecting TOOLSET > BASIC.

3. To work with AutoTitler, you can either create a template or use a pre-existing template. We'll modify a pre-existing Marquee template to fit our needs. In the Style Library, click the TEMPLATES tab as shown in Figure 9.40.

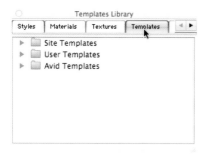

Figure 9.40
In the Style Library, click the Templates tab.

4. In the Templates tab, click the **+** sign (Windows) or disclosure triangle (Mac) for AVID TEMPLATES and then again for LOWER THIRDS. The list of lower-third templates is revealed.

5. Double-click the NAMETITLECOMPANY template from the list to open it. The NameTitleCompany template includes three places for text: name, title, and company name. Those don't exactly fit our cast and crew title requirements, and the text should be centered, so we'll fix those two problems.

6. All the objects in the template open with red selection boxes around them. Click and drag all the objects to the center of the screen as shown in Figure 9.41. Then click the background to deselect all the objects.

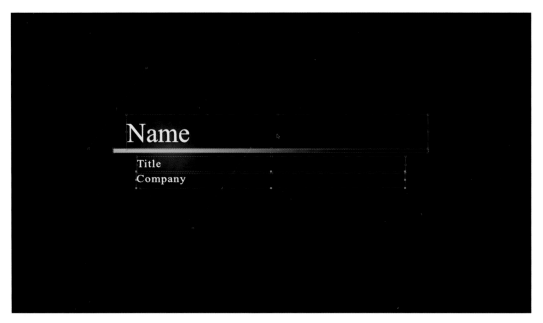

Figure 9.41
Click and drag all the objects to the center of the screen.

7. Choose VIEW > SAFE ACTION/TITLE.

8. To ensure that long names and titles will not be truncated, drag all text bounding boxes to the right edge of the safe title perimeter as shown in Figure 9.42.

Figure 9.42
Drag all text bounding boxes to the right edge of the safe title perimeter.

Note: If you started the title from scratch rather than use a pre-existing template, you need to rename each text layer Text Box 1, Text Box 2, etc.

9. In the Layers palette (found in the lower-right corner of the Marquee window), click the **+** sign (Windows) or disclosure triangle (Mac) next to LAYER 1. Notice that it lists a numbered text box for each line of text in your title. For AutoTitling, each text box is numbered from top to bottom, with the top line of text as Text Box 1 (see Figure 9.43).

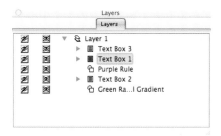

Figure 9.43
For AutoTitling, each text box is numbered, starting at Text Box 1.

10. To run AutoTitler, select FILE > AUTOTITLER. The Choose Input File for AutoTitler dialog box appears.

11. Navigate to DESKTOP > MC6 EFFECTS BOOK FILES > ADDITIONAL PROJECT MEDIA and select AUTOTITLER TEXT. Then click OK (Windows) or OPEN (Mac). The AutoTitler Preferences dialog box opens.

12. To process the files, click OK.

Note: Text files must be in the plain text (.txt) format for AutoTitler to read and load the file. To prepare a text file for lower thirds, open a text document. Type a name on the first line, press the Enter or Return key, and type the person's title on the second line. Press the Enter or Return key twice between this entry and the next. This tells the AutoTitler that a new entry is beginning.

13. A message box tells you when all possible titles have been created, and the last created title is displayed in the Monitor window. All the titles created by AutoTitler are now open in Marquee. You can view each title by choosing it from the Window menu. Select FILE > SAVE ALL TO BIN.

Tip: If the client or director changes his mind and wants a different look, with the AutoTitler it can be faster to regenerate the entire batch from a new template than modify each one.

Review/Discussion Questions

1. How do you open the Marquee Title tool?

2. What modifier keys are used as you drag a bounding box to increase the font size of a text object in the Marquee window?

3. True or false: To add a border around text, you enable the Border check box.

4. If you are defining a gradient, and the final colors on your title object's surface are not what you expect, what might you need to do?

5. Which tool is used to rotate objects on screen?

    a.

    b.

    c.

6. Which tab is used to make a texture more or less shiny?

    a. Style tab

    b. Surfaces tab

    c. Effects tab

7. Where are user styles found?

8. True or false: To add a keyframe on an animation curve, you click the curve where you want to add the keyframe.

9. What determines the duration of a quick fade in Marquee?

    a. The IN and OUT marks

    b. How the layer is trimmed

    c. The Quick Fade Duration window

10. What must the first text box be named for AutoTitler to work correctly?

Lesson 9 Keyboard Shortcuts

Key	Shortcut
E	Edit tool
T	Text tool
I	Mark IN
F2	Basic Layout
F4	Basic Animation Layout

Sliding Animation

In this exercise, you'll create new animated text for the opening title of our *Agent Zero* movie.

Media Used:

Agent MX-Zero

Duration:

20 minutes

GOALS

- Create a new *Agent Zero* title

Creating an Animated Title

1. Select CLIP > NEW TITLE to open Marquee.

2. Click the TEXT tool and type **AGENT**. Then create a new text box for the number **O**.

3. Align and center both text boxes so they appear to be typed on the same line as one word, AGENT0.

4. Add a gradient color to the number 0.

5. Add a texture with lighting to the AGENT text.

6. Set both text boxes to the TREBUCHET MS font.

7. Animate the **X** position of the AGENT text so it slides in from the right, and animate the **X** position of the number 0 so it slides in from the left.

8. Save the title and view it in the Source monitor.

Editing Titles into a Title Sequence

1. Load the **AZ PT2** MARQUEE**-START** sequence.

2. Locate three good locations after the main Marquee title you created.

3. Edit in the AutoTitler titles you created earlier in this lesson.

Using AVX Third-Party Plug-ins

After all the lessons in this book you should have a greater understanding of how to create some fundamental effects in Media Composer. This appendix will introduce you to a world of plug-in effects from other companies that can extend Media Composer's capabilities.

Media Used: Running the Sahara

Duration: 30 minutes

GOALS

- Learn about AVX
- Add Boris FX BCC plug-ins and AVX plug-ins
- Modify BCC plug-ins as segment effects
- Use BCC plug-ins as transition effects
- Use GenArts Sapphire plug-ins as segment effects
- Use GenArts Sapphire plug-ins as transition effects

About AVX

Avid Video Extensions (AVX) is software that enables other companies to develop effects that operate within Media Composer's Effect mode. The effects are called AVX plug-ins.

AVX plug-ins expand your creative palette with software from top visual effects designers, including Digital Film Tools, Noise Industries, and Red Giant Software.

You are able to create unique visual effects, animations, graphics, titles, and more with a broad collection of sophisticated compositing tools, 2D and 3D effects, motion tracking, image stabilization, effects, and transitions.

Adding Boris FX BCC AVX Plug-ins

Boris Continuum Complete (BCC) AVX is a comprehensive visual effects and compositing plug-in suite. It includes over 200 effects, including true 3D objects such as extruded text and spheres; particle effects to simulate rain, snow, or star fields; excellent keying and compositing tools; and a full suite of blurs, glows, and cinematic effects. All BCC AVX plug-ins take advantage of either multiprocessing or OpenGL hardware acceleration for an interactive effects design experience.

To use BCC plug-ins in Media Composer:

1. Start Media Composer and open the **RUNNING THE SAHARA** project.

2. From the Project window, open the **2 RTS SOURCE CLIPS** bin.

3. Locate the **RUNNER 1 INT** clip shown in Figure A.1 and edit four seconds of the clip into the Record monitor.

Figure A.1
Edit in four seconds of the Runner 1 INT clip.

4. Locate the **MAUR, SUNSET** clip shown in Figure A.2 and edit in four seconds after the runner clip.

Figure A.2
Edit in four seconds of the Maur, sunset clip.

5. From the **TOOLS** menu, select **EFFECT PALETTE**. When the Effect Palette opens, there will be 18 new categories for BCC at the top of the list. The category names describe the type of effects contained within them.

Note: To install a trial version of Boris Continuum Complete for AVX, go to www.borisfx.com and download the latest version. After you download and install the plug-ins, restart Media Composer, and you'll be able to follow these steps.

6. Click the **IMAGE RESTORATION** category shown in Figure A.3. There are 11 effects in this category that perform various fix-it–style operations on clips.

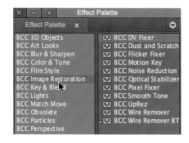

Figure A.3
Click the Image Restoration category in the Effect Palette.

7. Drag the **Smooth Tone** effect onto the runner clip in the Timeline. The Smooth Tone effect is used primarily for softening overly sharp or detailed images. It's great for softening wrinkly or uneven skin tones—like giving the talent a little extra "digital make-up"—as shown in Figure A.4.

Figure A.4
The Smooth Tone effect is primarily used for softening skin tones.

8. Place the position indicator over the runner segment and click the **Effect Mode** button. The Effect Editor opens with all the controls for the Smooth Tone effect.

9. In the Effect Editor, select the **Bypass** check box as shown in Figure A.5. This bypasses the effect, showing the original unaltered clip. It's a good way to compare the original with whatever change you have made in the effects.

Figure A.5
Select the Bypass check box to see the original image.

10. Deselect the **Bypass** check box and then select the **Launch Help File** check box. The help file for this particular BCC effect pops up in a PDF viewer. Both the Bypass and Launch Help File check boxes are available at the top of each BCC plug-in, making it easy to see and read what an effect does to the original image.

11. Close the PDF help file to return to the Smooth Tone plug-in in Media Composer.

12. Click the **No Preset** option just below the Launch Help File check box to launch a common control at the top of every BCC parameter list: a Preset menu. Depending on the flexibility and complexity of the particular plug-in, a number of presets are provided, allowing quick access to commonly used settings.

13. Choose **Smoother** from the **Preset** menu, as shown in Figure A.6. The actual amount of smoothness is determined by the Radius slider.

Figure A.6
Choose Smoother from the Preset menu.

Tip: Presets are a great way to start, but most of the time you'll want to customize the effect. After all, everyone has the same presets as you.

Modifying BCC Plug-ins as Segment Effects

Although Boris FX BCC plug-ins and other AVX plug-ins include presets, subtle adjustments to the major parameters of each effect can make it fit your shot even better.

To modify the preset you just added:

1. From the **Method** pop-up menu, choose **Smoother**. This gives the best quality but is slower to render than the default Faster setting.

2. Drag the **Radius X** slider to **20** as shown in Figure A.7. The skin on the man in the clip looks very plastic and unrealistic.

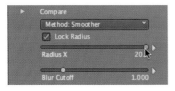

Figure A.7
Drag the Radius X slider to 20 to increase the smoothness.

3. Click the **COMPARE** disclosure triangle. The Compare menu that it reveals allows you to compare the original image with the altered image on screen. Instead of having to go up to the Bypass check box, you can select a Compare mode from the menu.

4. Choose **SIDE BY SIDE** from the **COMPARE** menu as shown in Figure A.8. A split screen display of the original image (left) and the smoothed image (right) allows you to make a before and after comparison while you make adjustments to the effect.

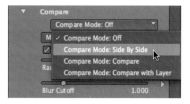

Figure A.8
Choose Side By Side from the Compare menu.

5. Choose **COMPARE** from the **COMPARE** menu. The Effect Preview monitor is now displayed with a purple line down the center. The half of the screen to the left of the line is the original image; the half to the right is the altered image, as shown in Figure A.9.

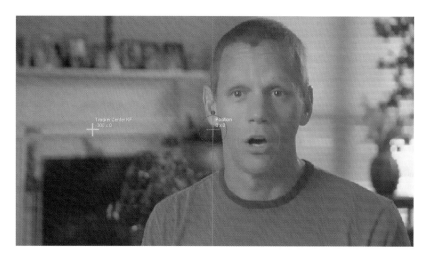

Figure A.9
Compare creates a split screen to compare the before and after results.

6. Hover the pointer over the line until it turns green; then click and drag the line until it is centered over the man's face, as shown in Figure A.10.

You are able to position the line anywhere in the image. As soon as you release the mouse, the screen updates to show the before and after at the new split point.

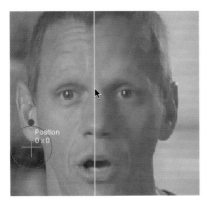

Figure A.10
Center the compare line over the man's face.

7. Drag the **RADIUS X** slider back to around **4.0**. This softens the man's face without removing too much detail.

8. To bring back even more detail, drag the **BLUR CUTOFF** to around **.40**. The Blur Cutoff will use luminance to bring the detail back into the highlights.

9. Lastly, Maximum Deviation can be adjusted in the Effect Editor but also directly onscreen. In the Effect Preview monitor, drag the **MAXIMUM DEVIATION** circle out to increase its radius until it says roughly **7.0**, as shown in Figure A.11. Increasing the radius of Maximum Deviation increases the radius or spread of the blur.

Figure A.11
Drag the circle on screen to increase the radius.

Tip: Onscreen widgets are available in most BCC plug-in effects, and control the parameters with the greatest impact on the image.

10. To view the clip without the onscreen controls, you can turn the widgets off using the fifth button from the top of the Effect Editor as shown in Figure A.12.

Figure A.12
Hide the onscreen widgets using the button on the side of the Effect Editor.

11. When you are done reviewing the effect, you can render it. Click the RENDER EFFECTS button at the bottom of the Effect Editor.

On the Web   The effects with "RT" at the end of their names play back in real time on certain Avid systems and do not need rendering. To find a list of real-time BCC effects or the system requirements, go to the Boris FX Web site.

You've added your first AVX plug-in. Many of the Boris FX BCC plug-ins use a layout similar to the one you just explored. Nearly all of them include a Preset menu at the top of the Effect Editor; the most common parameters are closer to the top and many have similar onscreen controls. You'll be able to use these skills as you explore more Boris BCC options. Next you'll look at a slightly different BCC plug-in that can be used as a transition effect.

Using BCC Transition Plug-ins

Boris Continuum Complete (BCC) AVX provides two methods to use effects as transitions. The easiest method is to apply a BCC Transition effect to a transition between two clips in the Timeline and watch the auto-animation happen. These transitions work just like standard Media Composer transitions but with more creative options. The second manual way is to use the BCC Two-Input effects. Since these effects do not auto-animate, you must keyframe parameter values to transition from the outgoing shot to the incoming shot. It won't be much of a lesson if Boris does all the work for you, so we'll take the road less traveled and use the Two-Input effects.

To create a Two-Input Transition effect:

1. Load the same sequence you used in the previous section.

2. Open the Effect Palette if it isn't already open and select the **BCC TWO-INPUT EFFECTS** category, as shown in Figure A.13.

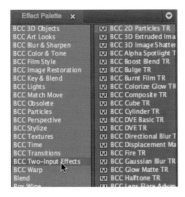

Figure A.13
Select the BCC Two-Input Effects category.

3. Drag **BURNT FILM TR** effect to the Timeline between the two clips in the sequence as shown in Figure A.14.

Figure A.14
Drag Burnt Film TR effect to the transition in the sequence.

4. Place the position indicator over the transition point and click the **EFFECT MODE** button. The Effect Preview monitor shows the effect at a midway point as shown in Figure A.15, but it's your job on a Two-Input transition to animate it.

Figure A.15
The Effect Preview monitor shows the effect at a mid-way point.

5. In the Effect Preview monitor position bar, drag to the start of the transition and click the ADD KEYFRAME button.

6. In the Effect Editor, drag the BURN AMOUNT slider all the way to the left until it is set to 0, as shown in Figure A.16. The Burn effect in the Effect Preview monitor goes away, and all you see is the runner clip.

Figure A.16
Drag Burn Amount all the way to the left, until it is set to 0.

7. In the Effect Preview monitor position bar, drag to the end of the transition and click the ADD KEYFRAME button again.

8. Drag the BURN AMOUNT slider all the way to the right until it is set to 1.0. The Maur, sunset clip is now displayed in the Effect Preview monitor.

9. To view the effect, click the PLAY button under the Effect Preview monitor. The runner clip now burns away to reveal the sunset clip.

You've added your first AVX plug-in. Many of the Boris FX BCC plug-ins use a layout similar to the one you've seen. Next you'll look at a slightly different AVX plug-in that can be used as a transition effect.

Using GenArts' Sapphire Plug-ins as Segment Effects

GenArts' Sapphire is another popular package of image-processing plug-in effects for use with Media Composer. It includes over 190 AVX plug-ins, each with parameters that can be adjusted for an almost unlimited range of results. Introduced in 1996, Sapphire plug-ins have become an industry standard for elaborate visual effects creation at leading studios, broadcast facilities, and postproduction facilities around the world.

Some of the most popular Sapphire effects are the lighting effects, which produce photo-realistic glows, light rays, sparkles, and more. Let's start with one of these.

To add a Sapphire Glow effect:

1. Using the same project and sequence you created earlier in this lesson, open the **2 RTS SOURCE CLIPS** bin.

2. Locate the **CAIRO PYRAMIDS** clip shown in Figure A.17 and edit four seconds into the sequence after the Maur, sunset segment.

Figure A.17
Edit the Cairo Pyramids clip into the sequence.

3. From the **TOOLS** menu, select **EFFECT PALETTE**. When the Effect Palette opens, the nine Sapphire effect categories are located near the bottom.

To install a trial version of GenArts Sapphire for Avid, go to www.genarts.com and download the latest version. Once you download and install the plug-ins, restart Media Composer, and you'll be able to complete the steps that follow.

On the Web

4. Click the **SAPPHIRE LIGHTING** category and drag the **S_GLOW** effect onto the pyramids clip in the Timeline. The S_Glow effect adds a very bright glow to the luminance, as shown in Figure A.18. It's nice by default, but it should look warmer and not be as overwhelming to the image.

Figure A.18
The S_Glow effect adds a very bright glow effect to the luminance part of image.

5. Place the position indicator over the pyramids segment and click the
   EFFECT MODE button. The Effect Editor opens with all the controls for
   the S_Glow effect.

6. The best way to start is by selecting a preset. At the top of the Effect Editor,
   click the **LOAD PRESET** button as shown in Figure A.19. The Preset browser
   opens to give you a great graphical way to select the preset you want.

Figure A.19
Click the Load Preset button at the top of the Effect Editor.

7. Click the **HEAT PASSION** preset in the lower half of the browser as shown
   in Figure A.20. Selecting a preset displays it in the larger preview window
   for a more detailed view.

Figure A.20
Click the Heat Passion preset in the lower half of the browser.

8. Click the **LOAD** button in the bottom-right corner of the Preset browser. The Preset browser closes, and the Heat Passion preset is applied to the segment in the Timeline. The parameters for all Sapphire effects are listed so that the general controls are closer to the top and the more detailed controls are lower in the Effect Editor.

Note: The treadmill wheel is a useful design for parameters with an unlimited range. You can move the mouse completely to the edge of the screen to add as much value to the parameter as you wish.

9. Drag the **THRESHOLD** slider slightly to the left until it is set to **.3**. The Threshold parameter determines how much of the image is affected by the glow. The lower you set the slider, the more midtones and darker areas are affected by the glow.

Tip: Anytime you are using a Sapphire lighting effect, look for the Threshold parameter. It's present in all lighting effects and is the parameter that controls how much of the shot is affected.

10. The S_Glow effect also has onscreen controls for adjusting the glow width RGB settings. Place the cursor over the inner white onscreen widget. The ring turns yellow to indicate that you can drag it.

11. Drag the white ring out to double its size as shown in Figure A.21. Increasing the width increases the spread of the glow.

Figure A.21
Drag the white ring out to double its size.

12. Drag the horizontal arrow on the widget circle to stretch it out slightly as shown in Figure A.22. As you adjust the arrow, the glow rings expand, creating an oval shape. The glow also expands horizontally on the screen.

Figure A.22
Drag the horizontal arrow on the widget circle to stretch it out slightly.

13. You can adjust the width of the individual RGB channels. Drag the red circle to make it larger than the other circles. The spread of the red glow in the image increases as you make the red circle larger.

14. To compare the altered image with the original, click the **BYPASS EFFECT** button at the bottom of the Effect Palette. Click the **BYPASS EFFECT** button again to return to the glowing image.

Note: If you select Bypass Effect and render the Sapphire plug-in, it will render as it is displayed, ignoring the effect. Be sure to turn the Bypass Effect option off before you render an effect.

As with the Boris BCC segment effect plug-ins, all the Sapphire plug-ins require rendering. Next, let's take a look at how you can apply Sapphire plug-ins as transition effects.

Using GenArts' Sapphire Plug-ins as Transition Effects

Sapphire plug-ins include over 50 transitions consisting of various dissolves and wipes that function just like standard Avid non–real-time transitions. This exercise will cover a swish pan–style transition to familiarize you with how they work.

To add a Sapphire transition effect:

1. Using the same sequence you used in the previous section, open the Effect Palette, if it isn't already open, and select the **SAPPHIRE TRANSITIONS** category.

2. Drag the **S_SWISHPAN** effect to the Timeline between the last two clips in the sequence as shown in Figure A.23.

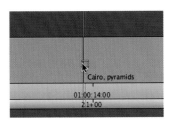

Figure A.23
Drag the S_SwishPan effect to the Timeline between the last two clips in the sequence.

3. Place the position indicator over the transition point and click the **EFFECT MODE** button. The Effect Preview monitor shows the effect at a midway point as seen in Figure A.24.

Figure A.24
The Effect Preview monitor shows the effect at a midway point.

4. To view the effect, click the **PLAY** button under the Effect Preview monitor.

5. Although there are no presets for this transition, you can adjust the blur amount and the direction. Choose **DIRECTION DOWN** from the **DIRECTION** pop-up menu as shown in Figure A.25.

Figure A.25
Choose Direction Down from the Direction pop-up menu.

6. Click the **PLAY** button under the Effect Preview monitor to see the changed direction.

Now that you've added segment and transition effects from two of the larger AVX plug-in vendors, you may want to try some of the many other third-party effects as well.

On the Web

To explore additional third-party plug-ins, open the Media Composer Marketplace menu and choose Video Plug-ins. Or, check them out online:

- **3Prong.** www.3prong.com
- **Digital Film Tools.** www.digitalfilmtools.com
- **New Blue Effects.** www.newbluefx.com
- **Noise Industries.** www.noiseindustries.com
- **ProDad.** www.prodad.com
- **Red Giant.** www.redgiantsoftware.com
- **StageTools.** www.stagetools.com
- **Tiffen.** www.tiffen.com
- **Ultimatte.** www.ultimatte.com

Performance and Rendering

As you work through the lessons in this book, you will likely find a point at which you are using are non–real-time effects, or your computer is unable to play all the real-time effects you added to a sequence. This lesson will help you understand the limitations of your system and teach you the various render options available, empowering you to work as efficiently as possible with Media Composer effects.

Media Used: Running the Sahara

Duration: 30 minutes

Note: This appendix assumes that you have Boris FX BCC plug-ins and GenArts Sapphire plug-ins installed. If necessary, see Appendix A, "Using AVX Third-Party Plug-ins," for installation instructions.

GOALS

- Identify and interpret Media Composer's performance indicators
- Adjust playback quality and performance
- Render individual effects
- Use ExpertRender to render effects selectively
- Control render quality
- Clear render links

Understanding Performance

All effects in Media Composer can be categorized into two categories: real-time and non–real-time effects. Visual effects use complex mathematical equations to produce their results. Real-time effects are designed to be calculated and displayed as they are played back. Non–real-time effects must be rendered to be played back.

Rendering is a process by which Media Composer calculates (or creates) the effect and writes the resulting image into a video file.

Note: Media Composer refers to effect render files as *precomputes*—files that have been computed, or calculated, in advance of playback.

Playing back a real-time effect can require tremendous processing power to do successfully. Playing back the render file, on the other hand, is just like playing any other media file and requires very little processing power. This is why rendering can greatly improve playback performance of complex sequences. The downside, however, is that you have to wait for the render to complete.

So before we render, let's examine how the system attempts to play media back in real time and what can be done to delay rendering until it's really necessary.

Understanding Real-Time–Effects Playback

Depending on your system configuration and related hardware, your playback performance will vary. No matter how powerful your computer system is, your imagination can outdo it. At some point, you will build effects that will need to be rendered to play back in real time. But why, if they are all real-time effects?

Media Composer uses a unique approach to playback, designed to play as many effects as possible in real time.

Rather than playing directly off of the hard drive, the Avid system always plays out of a special reserved area of the host computer's RAM. This reserved area, or buffer, can hold over 10 seconds of full-quality uncompressed video. When you click Play, the following happens:

1. The system immediately begins pulling frames of media off the drive, processing any effects, and loading the final result into this buffer. This process almost always occurs faster than real time. The less processing required for a frame, the more quickly it can load into the buffer. Indeed, if playing clips without effects, 10 seconds of media can usually be loaded into the buffer in a few seconds.

2. Once a minimum number of frames has been loaded into the buffer, playback begins.

3. After playback begins, the system continues to process frames in the sequence and load them into the buffer until the end of the sequence is reached.

Media Composer will do its best to keep the playback buffer full. When playing through clips without effects or even a few effects, the system is able to process the frames faster than real time, and the buffer stays full. But when it encounters a complex effect composite, the buffer may begin to empty. The longer the complex effect composite, the more likely the buffer may empty completely.

Because the buffer is empty, Media Composer must wait for frames to be processed before they can be played back. The result is dropped frames—frames of video that are skipped.

Note: When frames are dropped, the frame rate drops dramatically, but audio/video sync is always maintained.

Measuring Performance

You will probably notice if the system drops frames. It's clearly visible during playback and looks like the video gets stuck for a moment, or worse, it freezes for a second or two until the playhead moves past the stack of effects. You probably don't need any special indicator to tell you when frames are dropped. But how do you know when you're getting close to the breaking point?

Every time you play the Timeline, Media Composer is monitoring system performance. If it detects that the system is reaching its limits, it warns you using playback performance indicators. These display as a yellow, red, or blue bar on the timecode track and in the timecode ruler at the top of the Timeline.

To test your system performance:

1. Open the RUNNING THE SAHARA project.

2. Open the RTS PT2 FX SEQUENCES bin and load the RTS PT2 FX LESSON XB sequence.

3. Play the entire sequence from the beginning to the end. How did it do? Any performance bars in the timecode tracks?

Note: It may be necessary to adjust the Timeline zoom to see the performance bars.

Depending on the color, these bars show where the system either is being stressed
or is dropping frames. Figure B.1 shows an example of these performance bars.

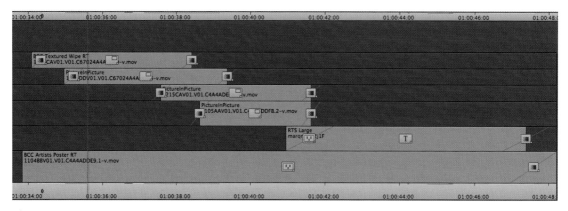

Figure B.1
Timeline performance bars.

- **Yellow bars.** These indicate areas that stressed the system—the CPU and
  GPU—during playback but did not cause it to drop frames.

- **Blue bars.** These indicate areas that stressed the drives on which the media
  was stored during playback but did not cause it to drop frames. If these bars
  occur frequently, you may want to move your media to faster drives or
  change your drive configuration (for example, to a RAID 0 configuration).

- **Red bars.** These indicate areas that overtaxed the system during playback.
  In these areas, the system dropped frames in order to play through the effect
  composite. The effects in these areas must be rendered to prevent dropped
  frames next time you play the sequence.

Even if your system was able to play the sequence in its entirety at the current
quality level, knowing that you stressed the system can help you decide, for example, if you need to render the Timeline before that important screening comes up.

If you stressed the system or dropped frames, you have two options: Adjust the
playback quality setting or render the effects.

Just Play Through It

Media Composer provides settings that enable you to adjust playback quality to
squeeze more real-time performance out of your system. The concept is simple:
It's easier and faster for the system to display a low-quality image—a sketch—of
the final effects composite than it is to process and display the full-quality image.

As an editor, it makes it easier to design complex effect composites if you don't have to stop and render until the very end.

Video Quality Menu

The Video Quality menu is located at the bottom of the Timeline and can be used to change the amount of processing that is done when playing back effects. Right-click the Video Quality icon to display the Video Quality menu, shown in Figure B.2.

Figure B.2
Video Quality menu.

The following video quality options are available:

- **Full Quality.** This option processes video at full quality with full-frame uncompressed video. Although it provides the best-looking images, it can significantly stress the system. Media Composer displays a solid green icon when this option is enabled.

- **Draft Quality.** This option scales the frame by 50% in each direction (or ¼ frame). This results in a slightly softer image but enables more effects to be processed in real time. This is the default quality setting. Media Composer displays an icon that is half yellow and half green when this option is enabled.

- **Best Performance.** This option reduces the media to process even further by scaling the image by 25% in each direction (or ¹⁄₁₆ frame). This results in a very soft image but enables maximum real-time–effects processing. Media Composer displays a solid yellow icon when this option is enabled.

Note: Depending on your video hardware configuration, you may also see a full quality, 10-bit option. This option increases the bit depth of the video being sent to your video hardware from 8-bit to 10-bit.

To see the impact of changing the video playback quality:

1. If it's not already open, load the **RTS PT2 FX LESSON XB** sequence.

2. Right-click the **VIDEO QUALITY** icon and select **FULL QUALITY**.

3. Play the sequence from beginning to end, taking note of the playback performance around the effect composites.

4. After playback is complete, examine the render bars.

5. Click the **VIDEO QUALITY** icon to toggle it to **BEST PERFORMANCE** (yellow/yellow).

6. Play the sequence again from beginning to end. Take note of how the performance improves and the image quality is reduced.

Most of the time, lowering the playback quality can enable you to complete your effects design work without rendering, but for playback at full quality, you will need to render. Like most things in Media Composer, there are a number of different render options and techniques. We'll explore these in the next section.

The Technical Side of Real-Time–Effect Playback Limitations

Many different things can affect real-time performance. Some limitations cannot be changed without replacing your system, but others can be worked around by either changing the way you work or reconfiguring your system.

System Performance

Media Composer uses an effects processing architecture called Avid Component Processing Library (ACPL). With ACPL, Avid is less dependent on dedicated effects hardware, as it leverages both the CPU and the graphics card (GPU) for maximum processing power. The Avid system automatically selects the most efficient and highest performance combination of processing elements, whether via CPU or GPU. This results in 300% to 400% faster effects processing than previous versions of Media Composer.

Because effects processing depends on the power of the host rather than dedicated hardware, determining the elements of system performance is critical. Several of these factors are listed here.

■ **CPU speed and configuration.** This affects performance because the faster and more efficient the processor, the more rapidly it can process effects. Avid strongly recommends using multiprocessor systems for the best possible performance. The CPU has two primary responsibilities: decompressing media and compositing effects. Depending on the effect and your system configuration, the GPU may also be involved in effect compositing, which lets the CPU focus on other things.

■ **RAM speed.** This is critical because video is played out of a RAM buffer rather than directly off the drives. RAM speed is affected by both the physical speed of the memory and the configuration of that memory. For example, the fastest systems use not only high-speed RAM but also pair, or interleave, the RAM chips. This process, which is similar to drive striping, allows even greater RAM speed.

■ **Overall system transfer speed.** This affects the ability to move media around the system. Several areas affect performance, including the system bus speed, the speed of your GPU, the use of PCIe cards, and the number of lanes allowed for data transfer. In addition, the way the system is designed can affect transfer performance. It is impossible to determine these bottlenecks without extensive system testing. This is why Avid tests and qualifies computer systems for use with their systems. For a complete list of qualified systems, refer to the system specifications on the Media Composer product page: www.avid.com/products/media-composer/hardware-options.

■ **Graphics card (GPU) performance.** This affects effect processing because both the CPU and the GPU are used for compositing. This hybrid relationship dynamically sends effects to be processed by each, so it is very important that your system is equipped with a qualified graphics card.

■ **Other running system processes.** System processes such as a music player can take processing cycles away from Media Composer and negatively affect real-time play-back performance. This is especially true of programs that are accessing the drives or moving large amounts of data across the system. For example, Norton AntiVirus real-time virus scanning checks files as they are accessed and will have some negative impact on playback performance. By the same token, rendering a composite in Adobe After Effects in the background will have a dramatic negative impact, as rendering heavily tasks the entire system.

Hard Drive Performance

Your hard drive configuration and drive type can definitely affect performance. If the system is displaying lots of blue performance indicators, you may need to change the way your drives are configured on your system.

■ SCSI and SAS drives provide excellent performance on Avid editing systems. In addition, their performance can be enhanced by striping multiple drives together. Striping dramatically increases performance and increases the number of streams possible. For the very highest possible performance, you should four-way stripe SCSI drives across two SCSI buses. *Striping* is a process where two or more drives are joined together by the system and treated as a single drive. By combining multiple drives, the system can read and write material much more quickly. Striping is available for all SCSI and Fibre drives. Some systems also support SATA drive striping.

■ Serial ATA (SATA) drives vary in performance and do not approach the performance of SCSI drives, even when striped. SATA drives are available at various performance levels, and a common metric is the drive speed, usually measured in RPM. It is strongly recommended that you use drives that run at 7,200 RPM or greater.

■ USB 2.0 and FireWire drives are essentially external SATA drives that connect by either a FireWire or USB 2.0 interface. Because of the limited speed of these connections, their performance usually is worse than internal SATA drives.

■ USB 3.0, eSATA, and Thunderbolt drives are also essentially external SATA drives, but they connect via a much faster interface. These drives potentially can run as fast as internal drives, but the performance is highly dependent on the drive inside the case.

■ Fibre channel drives provide a high level of performance but are rarely connected to a single workstation. Instead, these drives are typically attached to an Avid ISIS server.

Rendering Effects

Once you decide it's time to render, you'll also need to decide which effects to render. Depending on the situation, you may choose to render all the effects (such as for final output) or you may choose to render only certain effects (such as to review an effect composite at full quality for director or client approval).

When an effect is rendered, the render file always contains the composite of the effect rendered and all lower tracks and effects. This is the basic tenet of all rendering in Media Composer and a key consideration in how you choose to render the sequence.

Rendering Individual Effects

Sometimes all you really need to render is one effect. The simplest way to render a single effect is to use the Render Effect button in the Timeline, shown in Figure B.3.

To render an individual effect in the Timeline:

1. If it's not already open, load the **RTS PT2 FX Lesson XB** sequence.

2. Open the **Markers** tool from the **Tools** menu and double-click **marker 0001**. The position indicator will jump to that location in the Timeline.

3. Click the **Render Effect** button. All the effects on all clips at this position on active tracks will be highlighted for rendering and a Render Effect dialog box will open, as shown in Figure B.4.

Render Effect button

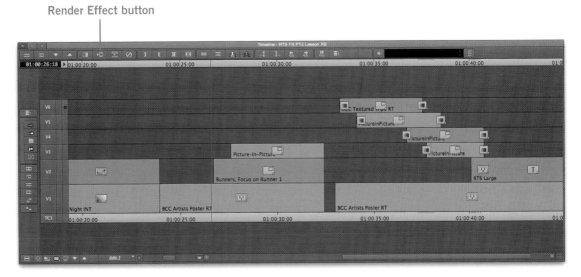

Figure B.3
The Render Effect button in the Timeline.

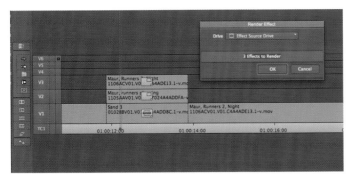

Figure B.4
All effects segments on active tracks selected for rendering.

Tip: The Render Effect button can be mapped to your keyboard. It is available on the FX tab of the Command palette. Using it from the keyboard is the same as clicking the button in any window. The function will be determined by whichever window is active.

4. Click **CANCEL**. Since the segment on V3 covers the same area as the segments on V2 and V1, we really only need to render V3. (Remember that a render always includes everything underneath it.)

5. Deselect **V1** and **V2**.

6. Click the RENDER EFFECT button again. This time only V3 is highlighted. (See Figure B.5.)

7. Select the drive to create the render files, also shown in Figure B.5, and click OK.

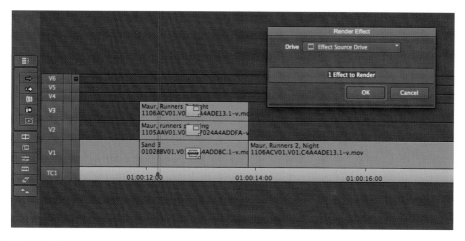

Figure B.5
The top segment selected for render, and target drive selected for render files.

Tip: You can immediately recognize when a clip has been rendered because the blue or green dot disappears from its effect icon. If the dot is still there, it hasn't been rendered yet.

Once an effect is rendered, it will remain rendered until you modify the effect. This includes moving the clips in a composite, since it changes the relationship of the frames that are being combined. In this case, that would mean moving the clip on V3. The good news is that if you accidentally break the render, you can undo. Media Composer will relink to the render file.

Rendering Multiple Effects

After building a more complex effects composite, you may want to render the entire group. This is easily done using IN and OUT marks to define the region.

Tip: Use this technique to render the entire sequence before final output. Simply set your IN and OUT marks at the beginning and end of the sequence, respectively.

To render multiple effects:

1. If it's not already open, load the **RTS PT2 FX LESSON XB** sequence.

2. Open the **MARKERS** tool from the **TOOLS** menu and double-click **MARKER 0002**. The position indicator will jump to that location in the Timeline.

3. Set an IN mark before the beginning of the sequence and an OUT mark at marker 0002.

4. Right-click in the Timeline and select **RENDER IN/OUT**, as shown in Figure B.6. All segments between the marks will be selected for render, and the Render Effect window will open.

5. Select the drive on which to create render files and click **OK**.

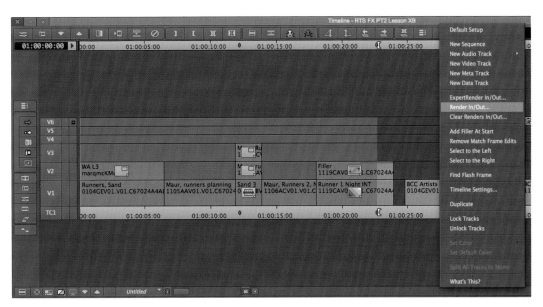

Figure B.6
Select Render In/Out to render all effects on active tracks in the marked region.

Note: The effect source drive listed in the various drive selection menus isn't one particular drive. Rather, it will place the render file on the same drive as the original source media. If the effect is a transition, this refers to the media on the outgoing shot.

Partial Renders

You can interrupt lengthy render processes by pressing Ctrl+. (period) (Windows) or Command+. (period) (Mac). Media Composer will ask if you want to save the partial render files. Any segments that were partially rendered will display a render bar—a red line at the top of the segment—indicating the portion of the effect that still needs to be rendered. See Figure B.7.

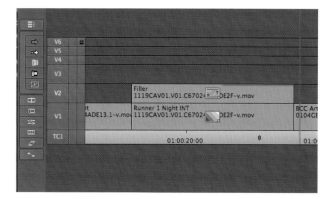

Figure B.7
The red render bar shows that V2 is partially rendered.

Using ExpertRender

In the previous section, you may have noticed that there was an ExpertRender In/Out menu option. ExpertRender is a feature designed to save you time in the render process, while ensuring that your system is capable of playing back all the effects in your sequence in real time. Like any automatic process in which decisions are made for you, it will do a great job sometimes and other times not so much.

First, ExpertRender uses your system's playback performance, as indicated by the performance bars, to determine what sections of the Timeline need rendering. Then it analyzes the effects within those sections using a couple of basic rules to determine which individual effects to render.

ExpertRender selects segments in the recommended ranges using the following rules:

- Render any effect that isn't completely covered by another effect that needs to be rendered.

- Render any non–real-time effects, unless completely covered by another effect that will be rendered. This includes nests that contain non–real-time effects.

Note: Media Composer is always "testing" your system playback performance,
       regardless of the playback quality setting in the Timeline.

To render a sequence using ExpertRender:

1. From the **RTS PT2 FX SEQUENCES** bin, load the **RTS PT2 FX LESSON
   XB** sequence.

2. Verify that all tracks are enabled and the video monitor is set to the top
   track.

3. Set the **VIDEO QUALITY** menu to **FULL QUALITY** (green/green).

4. Play the sequence, taking note of any areas where the system drops frames.

5. Mark an IN point at the beginning of the sequence and an OUT point at
   the end.

6. Right-click the Timeline and select **EXPERTRENDER IN/OUT**. The
   ExpertRender dialog box opens, as shown in Figure B.8.

Figure B.8
Select Render Recommended Ranges to
leverage your system's performance data.

By default, the **RENDER RECOMMENDED RANGES** option is selected. This
will render any effect segment where frames were dropped during playback
and the effects just before that location.

7. Select the drive on which to create the render files and click **OK**. The segments it is rendering are highlighted, and a window shows the progress of
   the renders. When complete, the sequence can be played back in real time.

Note: In the ExpertRender dialog box, the Render Entire Selection option will
       apply the logic of ExpertRender without taking into account your system's
       performance capability. This will result in a very conservative render selection
       and is only slightly faster than rendering all effects in the sequence.

The logic of ExpertRender errs on the side of caution, taking a conservative approach to how many effects need to be rendered. If you are going to play a sequence directly to broadcast from the Timeline, or are simply screening a scene for the client, Avid assumes that you'd rather spend an extra minute rendering than have the system hiccup during playback. But let's be realistic: Not every time you render is it for a high-stakes playback situation. As a result, there are times that you may wish to change the selection of ExpertRender.

Improving ExpertRender

As mentioned before, ExpertRender understands that if a segment is completely covered by a segment on a higher track that needs to be rendered, the lower effect can be skipped. But what if it sticks out a little bit, like the clip on V4, as shown in Figure B.9? Most of the effect is covered by another effect, but ExpertRender will want to render it completely.

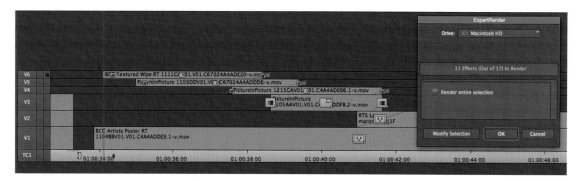

Figure B.9
ExpertRender naturally selects these effects for render.

Depending on how much the lower effect sticks out, you may be able to get away with rendering only the top effect. As usual, there is an easy way to override the automatic function.

To override the ExpertRender selection:

1. If it's not already open, load the **RTS PT2 FX Lesson** sequence.

2. Open the **Markers** tool from the **Tools** menu and double-click **marker 0003**. The position indicator will jump to that location in the Timeline.

3. Mark an IN mark before the first effect in this effect composite and an OUT point after the last effect.

4. Right-click on the Timeline and select **ExpertRender In/Out**.

5. Click the **Modify Selection** button. The ExpertRender dialog box disappears, but the effect segments remain selected in the Timeline.

6. Shift-click the segments on V1 and V2 to deselect them.

7. Click the **Render Effect** button in the Timeline. A Render Effect dialog box opens.

8. Select the drive on which to create the render files and click **OK**. All the selected segments are rendered.

Tip: Another way to improve ExpertRender's selection is to use the Add Edit command to divide a segment so the portion that sticks out is rendered by itself.

If you change the ExpertRender selection, it's always a good idea to test playback of the sequence when the render is complete—just to be sure you are still able to play all the effect composites in real time.

Controlling Render Speed and Quality

If you're like most editors, your first inclination is always to want the best quality possible. This produces beautiful images, but it's also the slowest way to go.

During the edit process, you may find yourself building complex effects and simply need a quick view of how well all the animated elements work together. Once all effects are finished, you can re-render at a high quality before showing the director or client.

This approach is often the most efficient way to work with effects-heavy sequences. There are two keys to this workflow:

■ Changing the render quality setting

■ Clearing existing renders to be able to re-render

Changing the Render Setting

The Render setting, found in the Settings pane of the Project window, has a number of options that control the quality of renders and image scaling, as well as the default render method used for motion effects.

To set the render quality for fast, draft-quality renders:

1. Open the **Render** setting from the Settings pane of the Project window. The Render Setting window opens, revealing several drop-down menus. The top one, Image Interpolation, controls the algorithm used to calculate effects, thereby controlling both the quality and the time it takes to complete.

2. Click the IMAGE INTERPOLATION menu.

3. Select DRAFT (NEAREST NEIGHBOR), as shown in Figure B.10.

Figure B.10
Use draft interpolation for "quick and dirty" renders.

With the system configured like this, all the effects will be rendered as fast as possible but at a lower image quality.

This is the ideal configuration when working on an effects-heavy sequence in which you will be doing numerous renders and want to minimize render time during the creative process. Before final output, you should re-render the effects at a higher quality setting.

To set the render quality for mastering-quality renders:

1. Open the RENDER setting from the Settings pane of the Project window.

2. Click the IMAGE INTERPOLATION menu.

3. Select ADVANCED (POLYPHASE).

Render Settings and Video Scaling

Media Composer lets you mix video of any size and format in the same Timeline. Any shots that don't fit the native format of the project will automatically be scaled to fit, and the frame rate will be adapted automatically to the project.

The Image Interpolation setting within Media Composer affects the quality of this scaling operation. For example, if you're cutting an HD project and have mixed in some SD video, Media Composer is capable of automatically scaling that to an HD image size at broadcast quality, but only if Image Interpolation is set to Advanced. If Image Interpolation is set to Standard or Draft, the quality of the upscaled SD images may be unacceptable.

Clearing Renders

Once an effect is rendered, Media Composer won't automatically render it again. This is a convenient feature most of the time. For example, suppose you've rendered several effects in the sequence, and you want to render the rest of the effects before output. You could simply render the entire sequence; no time will be wasted re-rendering any effects already rendered.

However, in this case you've rendered some effects at draft quality, and you want to re-render at mastering quality. The default behavior won't do at all. Not to worry, you can easily get around it with the Clear Renders command, which breaks the link between an effect and its render file, leaving the effect again unrendered.

Tip: If you accidentally clear renders on an effect that you didn't mean to, press Ctrl+Z (Windows) or Command+Z (Mac) to undo the action. Media Composer will relink the render file to the effect.

To clear renders:

1. If it's not already open, load the **RTS PT2 FX Lesson XB** sequence.

2. Mark an IN point at the beginning of the sequence and an OUT point at the end.

3. Enable all tracks, then right-click in the Timeline and select **Clear Renders In/Out**. A dialog box opens, as shown in Figure B.11. The default settings will protect the render files from any motion effects as well as any plug-in effects not installed on your system—a.k.a. "unknown effects." These would have been created by another editor sharing the sequence.

Figure B.11
The Clear Renders dialog box.

4. Click **OK**. All effects within the selected area of the Timeline will now be unrendered, ready for you to render at a higher quality.

Note: Clear Renders doesn't delete the render files, because you may be sharing that media with other editors. Be sure to go back and delete the precomputes (render files) for the project using the Media tool when the project is complete.

Congratulations! Armed with the knowledge you've gained in this lesson and this course, you can create a wide variety of effects in Media Composer. Just as important, you know how to manage system resources to work the most efficient way possible. In a world where time is money, this is a big advantage!

Glossary

Numbers

4:2:2 digital video   A digital video system defined by the ITU-R 601 (CCIR 601) technical documentation. 4:2:2 refers to the comparative ratio of sampling of the three components of the video signal: luminance and two color channels.

A

A-mode   A linear method of assembling edited footage. In A-mode, the editing system performs edits in the order they will appear on the master, stopping when the edit decision list (EDL) calls for a tape that is not presently in the deck.

add edit   An edit added between consecutive frames in a sequence segment within the Timeline. An add edit separates segment sections so the user can modify or add effects to a subsection of the segment.

AES/EBU   Audio Engineering Society/European Broadcasting Union. A standards-setting organization that defined a digital signal format for professional audio input to the Avid video-based editing systems using the SA 4 card. This signal format is typically used when you input sound directly to Avid video-based editing systems with a digital audiotape (DAT) machine, thereby bypassing the videotape capture process.

AIFF-C   Audio Interchange File Format-Condensed. A sampled-sound file format that allows audio data storage. This format is primarily used as a data interchange format but can be used as a storage format. OMF Interchange includes AIFF-C as a common interchange format for uncompressed audio data.

alpha channel   An 8-bit, grayscale representation of an image used to create a mask for keying images.

analog recording   The form of magnetic recording where the recorded waveform signal maintains the shape of the original waveform signal. Once the dominant format, analog recording is not common anymore due to the transition to digital formats. When captured, footage is converted from analog format to digital format.

anti-aliasing   A computerized process of digitally smoothing the jagged lines around graphic objects or titles.

aspect ratio   The numerical ratio of a viewing area's width to its height. In video and television, the standard aspect ratio is 4:3, which can be reduced to 1.33:1 or 1.33. The HDTV video format has an aspect ratio of 16:9. In film, some aspect ratios include 1.33:1, 1.85:1, and 2.35:1.

assemble edit   An edit where all existing signals on a tape (if any) are replaced with new signals. Assemble editing sequentially adds new information to a tape and a control track might be created during the edit. The edit is made linearly and is added to the end of previously recorded material.

Attic folder   The folder containing backups of your files or bins. Every time you save or the system automatically saves your work, copies of your files or bins go in the Attic folder, until the folder reaches the specified maximum. The Attic folder copies have the file name extension .bak and a number added to the file name. The number of backup files for one project can be changed (increased or decreased) in the Bin Settings dialog box.

audio timecode   Longitudinal timecode (LTC) recorded on an audio track.

AutoSave   A feature that saves your work at intervals you specify. Backups are placed in the Attic folder.

Avid disk   The disk that contains the operating system files. The computer needs operating system information to run.

Avid Projects folder   The folder containing your projects.

B

B-mode   A "checkerboard" or nonsequential method of assembly. In B-mode, the edit decision list (EDL) is arranged by source tape number. The edit system performs all edits from the tapes currently assigned to decks, leaving gaps that will be filled by material from subsequent reels.

B-roll   An exact copy of the A-roll original material, or new original material on a separate reel, for use in A-B-roll editing.

backtiming   A method of calculating the IN point by subtracting the duration from a known OUT point so that, for example, music and video or film end on the same note.

backup   A duplicate copy of a file or disk in another location.

batch capture   The automated process in which groups of clips or sequences, or both, are captured (recorded digitally).

Betacam   Trademarks of Sony Electronics, Inc. Two component videotape and video recording standards. Sony Betacam was the first high-end cassette-based system, recording video onto ½-inch magnetic tape. Betacam SP arrived three years after the first Betacam, improving on signal-to-noise ratios, frequency responses, the number of audio channels, and the amount of tape available on cassettes. SP is now the only type sold.

bin   A database in which master clips, subclips, effects, and sequences are organized for a project. Bins provide database functions to simplify organizing and manipulating material for capturing and editing.

black and code   Video black, timecode, and control track that are prerecorded onto videotape stock. Tapes with black and code are referred to as *striped* or *blacked* tapes.

black burst   A video signal that has no luminance or chrominance components (except burst) but contains all the other elements of a video signal. Black burst is the reference signal commonly used for timing audio and video samples.

black burst generator   An electronic device that emits a signal that registers as pure black when recorded on videotape.

black edits   1. A video source with no image. 2. A special source you can fade into or out of, or use for other effects.

bumping up   Transferring a program recorded on a lower-quality videotape to a higher-quality videotape (such as from ¾-inch to 1-inch videotape, or S-VHS to MII).

burn-in   A visible timecode permanently superimposed (burned in) on footage, usually in the form of white numbers in a black rectangle. Burned-in timecode is normally used for tracking timecode during previews or offline editing. A videotape with burn-in is also called a *burn-in dub* or *window dub*.

C

C-mode   A nonsequential method of assembly in which the edit decision list (EDL) is arranged by source tape number and ascending source timecode.

calibrate   To fine-tune video levels for maximum clarity during capture (from videotape).

capture   To convert analog video and audio signals to an Avid compressed digital signal format.

channel   1. A physical audio input or output. 2. One of several color components that combine to define a color image. An RGB image is made up of red, green, and blue color channels. In color correction, you can redefine color channels by blending color components in different proportions.

character generator   An electronic device, or computer device and software combination, that creates letters and numbers that can be superimposed on video footage as titles.

chroma   Video color.

chroma key   A simple effect that picks a color range and generates a matte from only those pixels.

chrominance   The saturation and hue characteristics of a composite video signal; the portion of the video signal that contains color information. Adjust chrominance and other video levels before capturing.

clip   1. A segment of source material captured into your system at selected IN and OUT points and referenced in a project bin. The clip contains pointers to the media files in which the actual digital video and audio data are stored. 2. In a record in a log, which stands for one shot, the clip includes information about the shot's start and end timecode, the source tape name, and the tracks selected for editing. 3. In OMFI, a general class of objects in the OMF Interchange class hierarchy representing shared properties of source clips, filler clips, attribute clips, track references, timecode clips, and edge code clips. A clip is a subclass of a component.

codec   *Co*mpressor/*dec*ompressor. Any technology for compressing and decompressing data. Codecs can be implemented in both software and hardware. Some examples of codecs are Cinepak, MPEG, and QuickTime.

color bars   A standard color test signal, displayed as a video pattern of eight equal-width columns ("bars") of colors. SMPTE color bars are a common standard. You adjust video levels against the color bars on your source videotape before capturing.

component video   The structuring of the video signal whereby color and luminance signals are kept separate from one another by using the color-subtraction method Y (luminance), B – Y (blue minus luminance) and R – Y (red minus luminance), with green derived from a combination. Two other component formats are RGB and YUV.

composite video   A video signal in which the luminance and chrominance components have been combined (encoded) as in standard PAL, NTSC, or SECAM formats.

composition   The standard term used by OMF Interchange to refer to an edited sequence made up of a number of clips. The OMF equivalent of a sequence in an Avid system.

compression   1. In audio, the process of reducing the dynamic range of the audio signal. 2. In video, a lack of detail in either the black or the white areas of the video picture due to improper separation of the signal level. 3. A reduction of audio or video (or both) signal detail to reduce storage requirements during transformation from analog to Avid digital format. In JPEG compression, for example, algorithms for variable frame length analyze the information in each frame and perform reductions that maximize the information retained. Compression does not remove any frames from the original material.

conform   To prepare a complete version of your project for viewing. The version produced might be an intermediate working version or the final cut.

console   A display that lists the current system information and chronicles recently performed functions. It also contains information about particular items you are editing, such as the shots in your sequence or clips selected from bins.

contrast   The range of light-to-dark values present in a film or video image.

control track   The portion of the video recording used to control longitudinal motion of the tape during playback. Control track can be thought of as electronic sprocket holes on the videotape.

CPU   Central processing unit. The main computational section of a computer that interprets and executes instructions.

crossfade   An audio transition in which the outgoing sound gradually becomes less audible as the incoming sound becomes more distinct. Also called an *audio dissolve*.

cue   To shuttle a videotape to a predetermined location.

cut   1. An instantaneous transition from one video source to another. 2. A section of source or record tape.

D

D1, D5   Two digital videotape recording formats that conform to the ITU-R 601 (CCIR-601) standard for uncompressed 4:2:2 digital component video. D5 is very similar to D1 in that it is a component digital recorder. However, D1 records with 8-bit accuracy; D5 records with 10-bit accuracy.

D2, D3   Two digital videotape recording formats for composite video. The main difference between the two is that D2 uses ¾-inch digital videotape, and D3 uses ½-inch digital videotape.

D-mode   An A-mode edit decision list (EDL) in which all effects (dissolves, wipes, graphic overlays) are performed at the end.

DAE   Digidesign Audio Engine. A trademark of Avid Technology, Inc. The application that manages the AudioSuite plug-ins.

DAT   Digital audiotape. A digital audio recording format that uses 3.8mm-wide magnetic tape in a plastic cassette.

decibel   dB. A unit of measurement for audio volume level.

deck controller   A tool that allows the user to control a deck by using standard functions such as shuttle, play, fast forward, rewind, stop, and eject.

depth shadow   A shadow that extends solidly from the edges of a title or shape to make it appear three-dimensional.

digital cut   The output of a sequence, which is usually recorded to tape.

digital recording   A method of recording in which the recorded signal is encoded on the tape in pulses and then decoded during playback.

digital television   DTV. The technology enabling the terrestrial transmission of television programs as data.

digitally record   To convert analog video and audio signals to digital signals.

dip   An adjustment to an audio track in which the volume gain level decreases, or "dips," to a lower level, rather than fading completely.

direct digital interface   The interconnection of compatible pieces of digital audio or video equipment without conversion of the signal to an analog form.

dissolve   A video or audio transition in which an image from one source gradually becomes less distinct as an image from a second source replaces it. An audio dissolve is also called a *segue*.

drop-frame timecode   A type of SMPTE timecode designed to match clock time exactly. Two frames of code are dropped every minute on the minute except the tenth minute, to correct for the fact that color frames occur at a rate of 29.97 fps, rather than an exact 30 fps. Drop-frame timecode is recorded with semicolons between the digits; for example, 1;00;10;02.

drop shadow   A shadow that is offset from a title or shape to give the feeling of spatial dimension.

dupe   Duplicate. A section of film or video source footage that has been repeated (duplicated) one or more times in an edited program.

dupe reel   A reel designated for the recording and playback of dupes (duplicate shots) during videotape editing.

DV   Digital video that is transferred through equipment conforming to IEEE Standard 1394. This equipment is sometimes called *FireWire* or *I-Link*.

DVE   Digital video effect.

dynamic range   An audio term that refers to the range between the softest and loudest levels a source can produce without distortion.

E

E-mode   A C-mode edit decision list (EDL) in which all effects (dissolves, wipes, and graphic overlays) are performed at the end.

EBU   European Broadcasting Union. A standards-setting organization in which only users (not vendors) have a voice.

edit   To assemble film or video, audio, effects, titles, and graphics to create a sequence.

edit rate   In compositions, a measure of the number of editable units per second in a piece of media data (for example, 30 fps for NTSC, 25 fps for PAL, and 24 fps for film).

EDL   Edit decision list. A list of edits made during offline editing and used to direct the online editing of the master.

effects   The manipulation of an audio or video signal. Types of film or video effects include special effects (F/X) such as morphing; simple effects such as dissolves, fades, superimpositions, and wipes; complex effects such as keys and DVEs; motion effects such as freeze frame and slow motion; and title and character generation.

energy plot   The display of audio waveforms as a graph of the relative loudness of an audio signal.

extract   To remove a selected area from an edited sequence and close the resulting gap in the sequence.

F

fade   A dissolve from full video to black video or from full audio to no audio, or vice versa.

field   One-half of the scan lines in an interlaced video frame. In most systems, the odd-numbered lines form one field, and the even-numbered lines form the second. NTSC video contains approximately 60 fields (30 frames) per second, and PAL video contains 50 fields (25 frames) per second.

file system   A way of organizing directories and files on a disk drive, such as FAT or NTFS for Windows computers.

filler clip   A segment of a sequence that contains no audio or video information. Filler can be added to the Source monitor (or pop-up monitor) and edited into a sequence.

format   To prepare a disk drive for use. For Windows computers, you format a disk drive by copying a file system (either FAT or NTFS) to the drive.

formatting   The transfer and editing of material to form a complete program, including any of the following: countdown, test patterns, bars and tone, titles, credits, logos, space for commercial, and so forth.

fps   Frames per second. A measure of the film or video display rates (NTSC = 30 fps; PAL = 25 fps; SECAM = 25 fps; Film = 24 fps).

frame   One complete video picture. A frame contains two video fields, scanned at the NTSC rate of approximately 30 fps or the PAL rate of 25 fps.

frame offset   A way of indicating a particular frame within the group of frames identified by the edge number on a piece of film. For example, a frame offset of +12 indicates the twelfth frame from the frame marked by the edit.

G

gain   1. A measurement of the amount of white in a video picture. 2. Audio levels or loudness.

gamma   A measurement of the midpoint in the luminance range of an image. Used in color adjustments to control the proportions of brighter and darker areas in an image. Also called the *gray point*.

gang   Any combination of multiple tracks that are grouped. An edit that is performed on one track is also performed on tracks that are ganged together.

generation   The number of times material has been rerecorded. The original videotaped material is the first generation. A copy of the original is a second-generation tape, and so on. Each generation shows a gradual loss of image quality. With digital copies, there is little or no loss in quality.

genlock   A system whereby the internal sync generator in a device (such as a camera) locks onto and synchronizes itself with an incoming signal. Using genlock to synchronize devices is most common in a studio environment.

gigabyte   GB. Approximately one billion (1,073,741,824) bytes of information.

H

handle   Material outside the IN and OUT points of a clip in a sequence. The Avid system creates handles when you decompose or consolidate material. The Decompose and Consolidate features can create new master clips that are shorter versions of the original master clip. The handles are used for dissolves and trims with the new, shorter master clips.

hard disk   A magnetic data recording disk that is permanently mounted within a disk drive.

hard recording   The immediate recording of all audio, video, timecode, and control tracks on a magnetic recorder. Because hard recording creates breaks in any existing timecode or control track on the tape, this procedure is often performed on blank tape when an edit is not required or in emergency circumstances. Also called *crash recording*.

HDTV   High-definition television. A digital video image having at least two times the resolution of standard NTSC or PAL video. The HDTV aspect ratio is 16:9. (Analog TV has a ratio of 4:3.)

head frame   The first frame in a clip of film or a segment of video.

headroom   1. In video, the room that should be left between the top of a person's head and the top of the frame when composing a clip. 2. In audio, the amount of available gain boost remaining before distortion is encountered.

hertz   Hz. The SI unit of frequency equal to one cycle per second.

hi con   A high-contrast image used for creating matte or luma keys.

hue   An attribute of color perception. Red, green, and blue form the color model used, in varying proportions, to produce all the colors displayed in video and on computer screens. Also called a *color phase*.

I

IN point   The starting point of an edit. Also called a *mark IN*.

initializing   The setting of the computer edit program to proper operating conditions at the start of the editing session.

interface   1. The computer software or hardware used to connect two functions or devices. 2. The program access level at which a user makes selections and navigates a given system.

IRE   A unit of measurement of the video waveform scale for the measurement of video levels, originally established by the Institute of Radio Engineers. The scale is divided into 140 IRE units, 100 above the blanking reference line and 40 below it.

ITU-R BT.601   The standard for standard-definition component digital video, published by the International Telecommunication Union as ITU-R BT.601-5 (formerly CCIR 601). This standard defines digital component video as it is derived from NTSC and PAL. It forms the basis for HDTV formats as well.

J

jam syncing   The process of synchronizing a secondary timecode generator with a selected master timecode.

JFIF   JPEG File Interchange Format. A file format that contains JPEG-encoded image data, which can be shared among various applications. JFIF resolutions store data at a constant rate; for example, JFIF 300 uses 300 KB for each frame it stores. JFIF resolutions comply with the ISO-JPEG interchange format and the ITU-R 601 standard.

JPEG   Joint Photographic Experts Group. Also, a form of compression developed by Avid Technology, Inc.

K

kerning   The spacing between text characters in print media, such as titles.

keyer   A procedural effect that generates a matte based on an algorithm and not a shape or mask that you create. Keyers can create transparency based on the luminance or chrominance in an image.

keyframes   A control point used to define the value of an effect parameter at a given point in time; changes between two keyframes are automatically interpolated by the system to create an animation of the effect parameter over time.

keying   To create transparency in a foreground image and combine it with a background image to create one composite image. To create a composite, you select a portion of the foreground that will be transparent. The transparent portion is called the *matte channel*.

kilobyte   KB. Approximately one thousand (1,024) bytes of information.

kilohertz   kHz. One thousand cycles per second.

L

layback   The process of transferring a finished audio track back to the master videotape.

layered tracks   The elements of an effect created by combining two or more tracks in a specified way, such as nesting one track as a layer within another.

leader   A length of film, tape, or a digital clip placed at the beginning of a roll, reel, or sequence to facilitate the cueing and syncing of material.

level   A quantitative measure of a video or an audio signal. A low level indicates the darker portions in video and the soft or quieter portions in audio; conversely, a high level indicates a brighter video image or a louder audio signal. The level of audio signal correlates directly with the volume of reproduced sound.

lift   To remove selected frames from a sequence and leave black or silence in place of the frames.

line feed   A recording or live feed of a program that switches between multiple cameras and image sources. Also known in sitcom production as the *director's cut*.

linear editing   A type of tape editing in which you assemble the program from beginning to end. If you require changes, you must rerecord everything downstream of the change. The physical nature of the medium (for example, analog videotape) dictates how you place material on the medium.

locator   A mark added to a selected frame to qualify a particular location within a sequence. User-defined comments can be added to locators.

log   To enter information about your media into bins at the beginning of the editing process. Logging can be done automatically or manually.

looping   1. The recording of multiple takes of dialogue or sound effects. 2. Continuous audio playback.

lossless compression   A compression scheme in which no data is lost. In video compression, lossless data files are usually very large.

lossy compression   A compression scheme in which data is thrown away, resulting in loss of image quality. The degree of loss depends on the specific compression algorithm used.

LTC   Longitudinal timecode. A type of SMPTE timecode that is recorded on the audio track of a videotape.

luminance   The measure of the intensity of the combined color (white) portion of a video signal.

M

mark IN/OUT   1. The process of entering the start and end timecodes for a clip to be edited into a sequence. 2. The process of marking or logging timecode numbers to define clips during a logging or capturing session.

master   The tape resulting from editing. The finished program.

master clip   In the bin, the media object that refers to the media files captured from tape or other sources.

master shot   The shot that serves as the basic scene, and into which all cutaways and closeups will be inserted during editing. A master shot is often a wide shot showing all characters and action in the scene.

match-frame edit   An edit in which the last frame of the outgoing shot is in sync with the first frame of the incoming shot, such that the incoming shot is an extension of the outgoing shot.

matchback   The process allowing you to generate a film cut list from a 30-fps video project that uses film as the source material.

matte channel   A portion of the foreground that is transparent, created through keying.

media   The video, audio, graphics, and rendered effects that can be combined to form a sequence or presentation.

media data   Data from a media source. Media data can be analog data (film frames, Nagra tape audio, or videotape video and audio) or digital data (either data that was captured such as video frame data and audio samples, or data such as title graphics, DAT recordings, or animation frames created in digital form).

media files   Files containing the digital audio or video data needed to play Avid clips and sequences.

megahertz   MHz. One million cycles per second.

mix   1. A transition from one video source to another in a switcher. 2. The product of a recording session in which several separate sound tracks are combined through a mixing console in mono or stereo.

mixdown audio   The process that allows the user to combine several tracks of audio onto a single track.

monitor   1. In video, a picture tube and associated circuitry without tuner or audio sections. The monitor includes the display of source media, clips, and sequences. In Avid products, virtual monitors are displayed on the screen in which source media, clips, and sequences can be edited. 2. In audio, to monitor specific audio tracks and channels, or another name for the speakers through which sound is heard.

MOS   The term used for silent shooting. From the quasi-German, *mit out sprechen*—without talking.

multicamera   A production or scene that is shot and recorded from more than one camera simultaneously.

multiple B-roll   A duplicate of the original source tape, created so that overlays can be merged onto one source tape.

multitrack   A magnetic tape or film recorder capable of recording more than one track at a time.

N

noise   1. In video, an aberration that appears as very fine white specks (snow) and that increases over multiple generations. 2. In audio, a sound that is usually heard as a hiss.

non-drop-frame timecode   An SMPTE timecode format that continuously tracks NTSC video at a rate of 30 fps without dropping frames to compensate for the actual 29.97-fps rate of NTSC video. As a result, non-drop-frame timecode does not coincide with real time. Non-drop-frame timecode is recorded with colons between the digits (for example, 1:00:10:02).

nonlinear   Pertaining to instantaneous random access and manipulation of any frame of material on any track and on any layer of an edit sequence.

nonlinear editing   A type of editing in which you do not need to assemble the program from beginning to end. The nature of the medium and the technical process of manipulating that medium do not dictate how the material must be physically ordered. You can use nonlinear editing for traditional film cutting and splicing, and for captured video images. You can make changes at the beginning, middle, or end of the sequence.

NTSC   National Television Standards Committee. The group that established the color television transmission system used in the United States, using 525 lines of information scanned at a rate of approximately 30 fps.

O

offline   Pertaining to items that are unavailable to the computer, such as offline disks or media files.

offline edit   The preliminary or rough-cut editing that produces an edit decision list (EDL).

OMFI   Open Media Framework Interchange, a registered trademark of Avid Technology, Inc. A standard format for the interchange of digital media data among heterogeneous platforms. The format is designed to encapsulate all the information required to interchange a variety of digital media, such as audio, video, graphics, and still images, as well as the rules for combining and presenting the media. The format includes rules for identifying the original sources of the digital media, and it can encapsulate both compressed and uncompressed digital media data.

online edit   The final edit using the master tapes and an edit decision list (EDL) to produce a finished program ready for distribution; usually associated with high-quality computer editing and digital effects.

OUT point   The end point of an edit, or a mark on a clip indicating a transition point. Also called a *mark OUT*.

outtake   A take that is not selected for inclusion in the finished product.

overwrite   An edit in which existing video or audio, or both, is replaced by new material.

P

PAL   Phase Alternating Line. A color television standard used in many countries. PAL consists of 625 lines of information scanned at a rate of 25 fps.

pan   An audio control that determines the left-to-right balance of the audio signal.

partition   A method of assigning disk space that creates two or more virtual disks from a single physical disk (similar to creating a directory).

patching   The routing of audio or video from one channel or track in the sequence to another.

pop-up monitor   An ancillary monitor used to view and mark clips and sequences.

position bar   The horizontal rectangular area beneath the Source monitor, Record monitor, Playback monitor, Composer monitor, and Source pop-up monitor that contains the position indicator.

position indicator   A vertical blue line that moves in the position bar and in the Timeline to indicate the location of the frame displayed in the monitor.

postroll   A preset period of time during a preview when a clip will continue to play past the OUT point before stopping or rewinding.

precomputed media   A computed effect stored in a file and referenced by a composition or sequence. Applications can precompute effects that they cannot create during playback.

preroll   The process of rewinding videotapes to a predetermined cue point (for example, six seconds) so the tapes are stabilized and up to speed when they reach the selected edit point (during capturing of source material from a video deck).

preview   To rehearse an edit without actually performing (recording) it.

progressive media   Media composed of single frames, each of which is vertically scanned as one pass.

project   A data device used to organize the work done on a program or series of programs. Bins, rundowns, and settings are organized in the Project window. The project bins contain all your clips, sequences, effects, and media file pointers.

R

RAM   Random access memory. Computer memory that is volatile and unsaved; information in RAM clears when the computer is turned off.

random access   The ability to move to a video point instantly, without having to shuttle.

real time   The actual clock time in which events occur.

reel   A spool with a center hub and flat sides on which magnetic tape is wound. Generally, a spool of tape is referred to as a *reel*, and a spool of film is referred to as a *roll*.

rendering   The merging of effect layers to create one stream of digital video for playback in real time.

replace edit   An edit in which a segment in the sequence is overwritten or replaced with source material of matching duration.

resolution   1. The amount and degree of detail in the video image, measured along both the horizontal and vertical axes. Usually, the number of available dots or lines contained in the horizontal and vertical dimensions of a video image. 2. The number of color or grayscale values that can be added, usually stated in bits (such as 8-bit or 24-bit). Sometimes dots per inch (dpi) is referred to as the *resolution*, although dpi is more properly called the *screen density*.

RGB   Red, green, and blue. In computer systems, the additive primary colors used to create all other colors on a computer monitor.

rough cut   A preliminary edit of a program, usually the result of an offline edit.

S

safe action area   A region of the video image considered safe from cropping for either the action or onscreen titles, taking into account variations in adjustments for video monitors or television receivers. Safe action is 90 percent of the screen measured from the center. Used in conjunction with the safe title area.

safe title area   A region of the video image considered safe from cropping for either the action or onscreen titles, taking into account variations in adjustments for video monitors or television receivers. Safe title is 80 percent of the screen measured from the center. Used in conjunction with the safe action area.

sample data   The media data created by capturing from a physical source. A sample is a unit of data that the capturing device can measure. Applications can play digital sample data from files on disk.

sample plot   The representation of audio as a sample waveform.

sample rate   The frequency of the sample units.

saturation   A measurement of chrominance. Saturation is the intensity of color in the video signal.

scale bar   A control in the Timeline window that allows you to expand and contract the Timeline area centered around the blue position indicator.

scroll bar   A rectangular bar located along the right side or the bottom of a window. Clicking or dragging in the scroll bar allows the user to move or scan through the file or window.

scrubbing   The process of shuttling through audio at various speeds as the audio pitch changes.

SECAM   Séquential Couleur à Memoire. A color television broadcast standard developed in France and several Eastern European countries.

segment   A section of a track or clip within a sequence in the Timeline that can be edited.

sequence   An edited composition that often includes audio and video clips and rendered effects connected by applied transitions. The Avid system contains a Timeline that graphically represents the edited sequence.

shot log   A listing of information about a roll of film or a reel of videotape, usually in chronological order.

shuttling   The viewing of footage at speeds greater than real time.

sifting   The displaying of clips that meet specific criteria in a bin.

silence   Blank (black) space in the audio tracks in a Timeline that contains no audio material.

SMPTE timecode   A frame-numbering system developed by the Society of Motion Picture and Television Engineers that is used primarily for electronic editing and timing of video programs. It assigns a number to each frame of video, telling the elapsed number of hours, minutes, seconds, and frames (for example, 01:42:13:26).

soft wipe   A wipe effect from one image to another that has a soft, diffused edge.

sorting   The arranging of clips in a bin column in numerical or alphabetical order, depending on the column the user selects.

source clip   One of the lowest-level building blocks of a sequence composition.

source mode   A method of assembly that determines in what order the edit controller reads the edit decision list (EDL) and assembles the final tape. There are five different types of source mode: A-mode, B-mode, C-mode, D-mode, and E-mode.

speed   The point at which videotape playback reaches a stable speed and there is enough preroll time for editing or capturing.

splice-in   An edit in which the material already on the video or audio track is lengthened by the addition of new material spliced in at any point in the sequence.

split   An edit in which the audio and video signals are given separate IN points or OUT points, so the edit takes place with one signal preceding the other. This does not affect audio and video synchronization. Also called an *L-cut*, *delay edit*, or *overlap edit*.

split-screen   The video special effect that displays two images separated by a horizontal or vertical wipe line.

stepping   The movement forward or backward one frame at a time. Also called *jogging*.

storyboard   A series of pictures (traditionally sketches) designed to show how a production will look. Comic books are essentially storyboards. Storyboards and subsequent sequences can be created by manipulating images from the captured footage in a bin.

streaming   A technology that allows users to watch a video clip or movie over the Internet while the video is being copied to their computers.

striped stock   Film stock to which a narrow stripe of magnetic recording material has been applied for the recording of a sound track.

subclip   1. An edited part of a clip. In a sequence, a subclip can be bound by any variation of clip beginnings, endings, and mark points. 2. Created by marking IN and OUT points in a clip and by saving the frames between the points. The sub-clip does not contain pointers to media files. The subclip references the master clip, which alone contains pointers to the media files.

synchronization   1. The pulses contained within a composite video signal to provide a synchronization reference for signal sampling. Also, a separate signal that can be fed to various pieces of equipment. 2. The sound recorded on a separate audio-tape but synchronized with videotape or film shot simultaneously. Also called *sync*.

T

tail frame   The last frame in a clip of film or a segment of video.

TBC   Time-base corrector. An electronic device that improves video signal stability by correcting time-base errors inherent in mechanical videotape recorders.

telecine   1. The process of transferring motion picture film to video. 2. Equipment used in the post-production process.

three-point editing   The basic principle that an edit event requires only three marks between the source and record sides to automatically calculate the fourth mark and complete the edit.

TIFF   Tag Image File Format. A tag-based system developed by Aldus Corporation for storing and interchanging raster images. The OMF Interchange standard includes TIFF as a common format for graphic interchange, and it includes TIFF with extensions as a common format for video frame data.

time-of-day timecode   The timecode that approximately matches the actual time of day (clock time).

timecode   An electronic indexing method used for editing and timing video programs. Timecode denotes hours, minutes, seconds, and frames (00:00:00:00) elapsed on a videotape. Address track timecode is recorded simultaneously with the video picture. Longitudinal timecode (LTC) is recorded on an audio track. Vertical interval timecode (VITC) is recorded in the vertical blanking interval of the video track. SMPTE timecode is the prevalent standard. Other timecodes exist that include film timecode and audio timecode used during film projects. During editing, the Avid system can display and track several types of timecode.

Timeline   The graphical representation of every macroscopic and microscopic edit made to a sequence, including all nested effects and layered tracks.

title bar   Located at the top of a window, it contains the name given to a project or bin.

tone   A constant audio frequency signal recorded at the start of a tape at 0 VU (volume units) to provide a reference for later use. Usually recorded in conjunction with color bars.

track   1. The section of tape on which a signal is recorded. Also called a *channel*. 2. The sound portion of a video program. 3. A region of a clip or sequence on which audio or video is placed. 4. A playback channel represented in a sequence as either a video track or an audio track. Tracks are composed of one or more segments connected by transitions.

track selector   A method of selecting one of the tracks from a track group; only the selected track is to be played. For example, a track selector can indicate which of four alternate views of the same scene is to be played.

tracking   The positioning of video heads during tape playback so that the heads reproduce the strongest possible signal. Tracking is adjusted on the deck prior to capturing.

transition   A representation of what is to take place as one segment ends and the next one begins. The simplest transition is a cut, which occurs in video when the first frame of the starting segment directly follows the last frame of the segment that is ending.

transition effect   A wipe, dissolve, or digital video effect (DVE) applied to an edit transition.

trim   The process of adjusting transitions in a sequence from the Timeline.

U

uncompressed video   A captured video stream that is not processed by a data compression scheme. The video signal remains uncompressed at all stages of the process: input, storage, and output. Uncompressed video conforms to the ITU-R BT.601 standard.

undo/redo   The process that allows a return to the state immediately preceding the last edit or a repeat of an "undo" edit.

up cut   In editing, to cut the end of the previous scene, often by mistake. In general, to cut short.

V

VCR   Videocassette recorder. A video recorder that uses consumer-grade video-tape formats such as VHS, Betamax, and Hi8.

vectorscope   A visual display that shows the electronic pattern of the color portion of the video signal. It is used to adjust the color saturation and hue by using a stable color reference such as color bars.

VHS   Video Home System. The ½-inch videocassette format developed by JVC for consumer and industrial use.

video   1. The visual portion of a program or sequence. 2. All television other than broadcast television.

video stream   1. In analog editing systems, also called a *video playback source*. 2. In digital editing systems, a stream of data making up a digital video image.

VITC   Vertical interval timecode. The timecode inserted in the vertical blanking interval.

volume level   An objective measure of audio intensity.

VU meter   Volume unit meter. An instrument used to measure audio levels.

W–Y

WAVE   RIFF Waveform Audio File Format. A widely used format for audio data. OMF Interchange includes it as a common interchange format for audio data.

waveform   1. In video, a visual display that shows the electronic pattern of the video signal. It is used to adjust the setup and gain by using a stable reference such as color bars. The Avid waveform uses a single-line display. 2. In audio, a visual representation of changing frequencies.

white point   The luminance value in a video image that you set equal to reference white when making a color adjustment.

wild sound   A recording of sound on either videotape or audiotape made without an accompanying picture. Also called a *wild track*.

YUV   The letter designations for luminance, luminance minus red, and luminance minus blue. YUV are the luminance and color difference signals of the component video standard for PAL. Also called *YCrCb*.

Answers to Review/Discussion Questions

Lesson 1 Answers

1. Under the Tools menu

2. c

3. False. All AudioSuite plug-ins require rendering. RTAS plug-ins are real-time plug-ins.

4. To smooth out volume changes on a segment

5. False. AudioSuite plug-ins can operate on segments in a sequence or master clips in a bin.

6. b

Lesson 2 Answers

1. The Quick Transition button is located in the Timeline toolbar. The default shortcut key is the backslash (\) key.

2. You identify the cuts in the Timeline by adding an IN point just before the first cut that will receive a Dissolve transition and an OUT point just after the last cut that will receive a Dissolve transition.

3. The three different effect types are transition effects, segment effects, and motion effects. Transition effects are applied at the cut point between two clips. Segment effects are applied to an entire clip within a sequence. Motion effects are applied to entire clips within a sequence or source clips to vary the frame rate of the footage.

4. Handle is extra media on a clip, beyond what is edited into a sequence. It is used to create a transition.

5. Make sure the V track is enabled and that no audio tracks are enabled in the Track Selector panel.

6. True

7. True

8. False. To save an effect template, you drag the effect icon from the upper-left corner of the Effect Editor into a bin.

9. You must click the Transition Manipulation button before dragging transitions in the Timeline.

10. To select segments when adding multiple segment effects, you must first click a Segment Mode button in the Smart tool.

Lesson 3 Answers

1. In the Effect Preview monitor, the Resize effect displays a white frame outline with resize handles. The handle in the upper-right corner is used to maintain the aspect ratio when you scale.

2. The position bar located under the Effect Preview monitor represents the duration of the segment the effect is on.

3. In the Effect Editor, click the enable buttons for Scaling and Position. Disabling parameter groups in the Effect Editor is a good way to compare the results with the original video.

4. You can increase the size of the outer yellow search rectangle to increase the area where the tracker will look for the tracking data point. This is helpful if the object you are tracking is moving too fast across the frame.

5. In the tracking parameters, click the enable button for the first tracker labeled "No Tracker." Enabling this tracker automatically assigns the tracking data point from the Tracking window to the Blur effect's shape.

6. The Enlarge button zooms in on the image in the Effects Preview monitor, while the Reduce button zooms out.

7. The Illusion FX category

Lesson 4 Answers

1. Freeze frames, Motion effects, and Timewarps

2. a

3. If the render type is not set correctly, you can end up with a lower-resolution result, visible flicker within what was supposed to be a frozen frame, or a softer image.

4. a

5. In a Motion effect, you specify the rate of the effect; with Fit to Fill, you specify the amount of source material to use within a defined duration in the Timeline.

6. b

7. Their rendering method can be changed without re-creating the effect; they can easily be modified to change the frame that is frozen, which can help avoid problems that may be encountered in later stages of post production; they are much easier to run and therefore much easier for the online editor to troubleshoot and correct problems.

8. Linear, Spline, Bézier, and Shelf

9. Shelf

Lesson 5 Answers

1. A scene was shot with multiple cameras of different makes and captured the images a bit differently; a scene was shot with one or more cameras not properly white balanced; the camera's auto-correction circuits inadvertently "fixed" a scene improperly, and what was recorded does not match what the subject really looks like; the cameraman deliberately captured the scene with low contrast so he could capture the maximum grayscale, expecting that the shot would be "fixed in post"; and the director or editor wants a shot to have a specific look that could not be captured in the camera.

2. Because the tonal range is the foundation of the image. It is not possible to achieve a good-looking image unless the tonal range is correct.

3. They are the defined limits for the grayscale within the digital video standards. Blacks should not go below video black or your program may be rejected by a broadcaster.

4. A response curve that defines how the tonal range transitions between black and white

5. To create a sepia tone, you add red and remove blue (which adds yellow).

6. The Safe Color Limiter effect is designed to prevent the grayscale from exceeding video white and video black and to ensure that the color does not exceed the limits typically allowed by broadcasters.

7. In the HSL group, you apply Auto Contrast and then Auto Balance, whereas in the Curves group, you apply Auto Balance and then Auto Contrast.

8. It allows you to identify a neutral tone in the image and create an additional point on each curve to correct for any color shifts that result from strictly balancing the red, green, and blue channels.

Lesson 6 Answers

1. Alt-drag (Windows) or Option-drag (Mac) an effect on top of the existing effect.

2. Autonesting

3. Simple nesting and expanded nesting

4. The video monitor follows you as you travel into the nest so you are able to see what is happening at a given level of the nest without seeing the effects above that level.

5. You always see the composited result of all effects in the nest regardless of where you are within the nest; you can hear audio when you play; you can access material before and after your effect nest.

6. Click and drag the effect icon in the Effect Editor for the effect you wish to reorder.

7. The Mask effect

Lesson 7 Answers

1. The Picture-in-Picture effect is a layering effect, allowing you to create multilayer composites from clips on multiple video tracks. Resize is a single-layer effect that is not designed for building multilayer composites.

2. Blanking is not designed to be seen. The black edges should not be part of an image used in a multilayer composite.

3. To create an image with a different aspect ratio, such as a wide bar or an image taller than it is wide

4. The first keyframe establishes the start of the move, while the second establishes the end. Without these two keyframes, the animation would not occur.

5. It reverses the order of all keyframes in an effect so that any animation plays backward. For example, if a PIP were animated to fly from right to left, reversing it would make it fly from left to right.

6. Ctrl+Shift

7. Keyframes are added to all parameters.

8. This command removes unnecessary keyframes and makes further keyframe manipulation easier.

9. An ease-in/out is added to every keyframe, making the motion smoother and more natural.

10. PIP is a two-input effect and has both a foreground and a background. Both of these are visible within the nest.

11. You can change the fill for the title by editing a different clip onto V2.

12. Nest when you want to add an element to another element or modify that element.

13. Layer when you want to add another element to a multilayer effect design.

14. To change the aspect ratio of the sequence

Lesson 8 Answers

1. c

2. True

3. A green or blue screen clip should be edited on the track directly above your background segment. In this example, the green screen should be edited onto track V3.

4. Left and right crop

5. False. A garbage mask is used to remove unwanted portions from the outer areas of the frame. The keyer is used to remove the remaining green/blue screen that immediately surrounds the subject.

6. To see the imperfections of a matte more clearly

Lesson 9 Answers

1. Select Clip > New Title and then click Marquee in the dialog box that appears.

2. Shift+Alt (Windows) or Shift+Option (Mac)

3. False. There is no Border check box. To add a border, you enable the Change Edge Properties check box in the Quick Titles window. Then choose an edging style from the pop-up menu.

4. Deselect Tint.

5. c

6. b

7. All styles are found in the Library tab. If the Library tab is not displayed, select Window > Library > Styles.

8. False. To add a keyframe, you right-click (Windows) or Control-click (Mac) on the animation curve and select Insert Key from the pop-up menu.

9. a

10. The first text box must be named Text Box 1.

INDEX

Notes

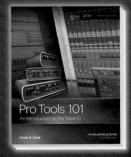

Notes

License Agreement/Notice of Limited Warranty

By opening the sealed disc container in this book, you agree to the following terms and conditions. If, upon reading the following license agreement and notice of limited warranty, you cannot agree to the terms and conditions set forth, return the unused book with unopened disc to the place where you purchased it for a refund.

License:

The enclosed software is copyrighted by the copyright holder(s) indicated on the software disc. You are licensed to copy the software onto a single computer for use by a single user and to a backup disc. You may not reproduce, make copies, or distribute copies or rent or lease the software in whole or in part, except with written permission of the copyright holder(s). You may transfer the enclosed disc only together with this license, and only if you destroy all other copies of the software and the transferee agrees to the terms of the license. You may not decompile, reverse assemble, or reverse engineer the software.

Notice of Limited Warranty:

The enclosed disc is warranted by Course Technology to be free of physical defects in materials and workmanship for a period of sixty (60) days from end user's purchase of the book/disc combination. During the sixty-day term of the limited warranty, Course Technology will provide a replacement disc upon the return of a defective disc.

Limited Liability:

THE SOLE REMEDY FOR BREACH OF THIS LIMITED WARRANTY SHALL CONSIST ENTIRELY OF REPLACEMENT OF THE DEFECTIVE DISC. IN NO EVENT SHALL COURSE TECHNOLOGY OR THE AUTHOR BE LIABLE FOR ANY OTHER DAMAGES, INCLUDING LOSS OR CORRUPTION OF DATA, CHANGES IN THE FUNCTIONAL CHARACTERISTICS OF THE HARDWARE OR OPERATING SYSTEM, DELETERIOUS INTERACTION WITH OTHER SOFTWARE, OR ANY OTHER SPECIAL, INCIDENTAL, OR CONSEQUENTIAL DAMAGES THAT MAY ARISE, EVEN IF COURSE TECHNOLOGY AND/OR THE AUTHOR HAS PREVIOUSLY BEEN NOTIFIED THAT THE POSSIBILITY OF SUCH DAMAGES EXISTS.

Disclaimer of Warranties:

COURSE TECHNOLOGY AND THE AUTHOR SPECIFICALLY DISCLAIM ANY AND ALL OTHER WARRANTIES, EITHER EXPRESS OR IMPLIED, INCLUDING WARRANTIES OF MERCHANTABILITY, SUITABILITY TO A PARTICULAR TASK OR PURPOSE, OR FREEDOM FROM ERRORS. SOME STATES DO NOT ALLOW FOR EXCLUSION OF IMPLIED WARRANTIES OR LIMITATION OF INCIDENTAL OR CONSEQUENTIAL DAMAGES, SO THESE LIMITATIONS MIGHT NOT APPLY TO YOU.

Other:

This Agreement is governed by the laws of the State of Massachusetts without regard to choice of law principles. The United Convention of Contracts for the International Sale of Goods is specifically disclaimed. This Agreement constitutes the entire agreement between you and Course Technology regarding use of the software.